THE
GOD
WINK
EFFECT

7 SECRETS TO GOD'S SIGNS, WONDERS, AND ANSWERED PRAYERS

SQUIRE RUSHNELL
& LOUISE DUART

HOWARD BOOKS
AN IMPRINT OF SIMON & SCHUSTER, INC.

NEW YORK   NASHVILLE   LONDON   TORONTO   SYDNEY   NEW DELHI

Howard Books
An Imprint of Simon & Schuster, Inc.
1230 Avenue of the Americas
New York, NY 10020

First Howard Books hardcover edition July 2017

HOWARD and colophon are trademarks of Simon & Schuster, Inc.

For information about special discounts for bulk purchases, please contact Simon & Schuster Special Sales at 1-866-506-1949 or business@simonandschuster.com.

The Simon & Schuster Speakers Bureau can bring authors to your live event. For more information or to book an event, contact the Simon & Schuster Speakers Bureau at 1-866-248-3049 or visit our website at www.simonspeakers.com.

Manufactured in the United States of America

10 9 8 7 6 5 4 3 2 1

Library of Congress Cataloging-in-Publication Data is available.

ISBN 978-1-5011-1957-6
ISBN 978-1-5011-1966-8 (ebook)

CONTENTS

THE GODWINK EFFECT

INTRODUCTION

What's a Godwink?

You've experienced Godwinks. We all have.

Godwinks are those little events that defy human understanding. In the beginning you were tempted to call them coincidences, but inwardly you sensed there was something more going on—and that God had something to do with it.

- Perhaps you seemed to randomly encounter someone who unexpectedly led you to a new career path or to the person you ended up marrying!
- Perhaps you picked up the phone and heard the voice of an old friend on the line, someone you hadn't heard from in years but had just been thinking about!

- Perhaps you have seen several important details of your life mysteriously align to converge perfectly on the same day or even at the exact same time!

When I introduced the term *Godwinks* in my first book, *When God Winks,* some fifteen years ago, it filled a vacancy in the English language. After all, if there's no coincidence to coincidence, what do you call it?

As a word-of-mouth phenomenon, *Godwinks* entered our language, moved from person to person, and even caught the attention of dictionary publishers.

It soon became apparent that people were using the word *Godwink* to express a new term: there is no word for "answered prayer," so people were saying, "I just had a Godwink!" when their prayer was answered.

From that moment, Godwinks and prayer became inextricably linked.

WHAT'S THE GODWINK EFFECT?

An *effect* is a change that results from an action or cause.

As a child you were fascinated to learn that a pebble tossed into a pond will cause multiple ripples upon the water.

The Godwink Effect is the series of ripples that result from Godwinks dropping wondrously into your life.

While it is special and comforting to think of every Godwink as an exclusive communication directly from God to you, out of seven billion people on the planet, God's blessings usually have more than one purpose or person in mind. Therefore, an initial Godwink frequently results in multiple outcomes, even producing a cascade of Godwinks that can lift you and many others.

Let us say you have been praying for a job. Nothing has panned out. You're feeling discouraged. But you don't give up. You just keep praying and trying.

Then something totally unexpected and illogical happens. For no real reason you take a different route to get somewhere, and you encounter someone who just "happens" along. A Godwink. That person not only assists you, but during the conversation finds out about your career qualifications and in turn connects you with a friend who is looking for someone with your exact skill set. Another Godwink. Before you know it, you have a new job, which, in turn, leads to a wonderful Godwink—meeting the love of your life—and your entire existence continues to change for the better. And it all started with one Godwink that rippled to many others.

Far-fetched?

Ask ten people if something like I just described has happened to them. My guess is most will say yes.

SECRET #1

PRAY

---

*Godwinks and prayer are inextricably linked.
When you pray more, you experience more
Godwinks. The best prayer is intentional, but God
occasionally proves He can hear your heart by
answering unintentional or even unasked prayers.*

DOUBT

In the beginning I was feeling uncertain.

Who was I to be spouting this thesis about Godwinks? I'm
not a theologian, a philosopher, or a scholar. I'm merely a TV executive. Just one of the guys who brought you *Schoolhouse Rock*.

But then I came across a statement that gave me encouragement, a statement by seventeenth-century religious leader Sir William Temple:

> *When I pray,*
> *coincidences happen.*
> *When I don't,*
> *they don't!*

I'm not alone! I thought.

Sir William lifted my spirits by validating my theory that Godwinks are connected to prayer. And this notion existed not just in my head but was held by others!

Of course I now joke that I can't fault the knighted evangelist for failing to use the proper word—*Godwink* instead of *coincidence*. The word wasn't around in the 1600s.

But I do enjoy paraphrasing Sir William:

> *When I pray,*
> *Godwinks happen.*
> *When I don't,*
> *they don't.*

So, in partnership with Sir William, we would like to introduce you to the first of Seven Secrets to God's Signs, Wonders, and Answered Prayers.

The first secret, very simply, is . . . *pray*.

When you *pray*, you clear the way for blessings that are waiting to be released. More prayer, more power. Less prayer, less power. Prayer is mysteriously related to the rate of Godwinks that flow into your life.

YOUR COMMUNICATION WITH HIM

Simply put, prayer is communication between you and God. You can talk to Him anytime from anywhere about anything, and you can talk to God much the way you would chat with a dear grandfather whom you admire and respect, who hangs on your every word, and who wants to know everything about everything you're doing, about what excites you and what concerns you.

One difference between your grandfather and God, though, is that the latter can literally move mountains and earth to comfort you, protect you, inspire you, and guide you to where you need to go.

GOD'S COMMUNICATION TO YOU

God hardly ever speaks to us in an out-loud, human voice. It happens, but very rarely.

Instead, sometimes you hear an inner voice that seems as clear and as distinct as the words to a song inside your head. That's infrequent as well.

More commonly, you feel a powerful inner sense that you need to do something—go check on the baby, watch that car that's coming from another direction, say something specific to a specific someone.

For most people, however, the most frequent form of direct, person-to-Person communication from God happens through Godwinks. Why not? Why wouldn't God use a nonverbal and totally amazing way to communicate to let you know that it's Him?

As you develop the ability to see Godwinks all around you, you'll see more and more of them more and more often. For Louise and me, it is now rare that we don't see Godwinks several times a day.

INTENTIONAL PRAYER

Intentional prayer is the best kind of prayer: you intentionally speak with God about a very specific need or issue. That's what Kate Hughes did, and her astonishing story will touch most of us. One medical issue after another drained her bank account, tested her stamina, and gave her a stage on which to demonstrate that when you engage in daily intentional prayer, God listens to you.

If you don't already agree, Kate's story may change your thinking.

Kate's Godwinks and the Wedding

Kate sat on the couch, opening mail. One envelope was plump and clearly of a high-quality paper. She carefully opened it.

As if it were a precious treasure map, she held the wedding invitation with both hands. It was beautiful. The raised lettering, in script, announced that in about a month her son, James, would marry his fiancée, Dana, in Sedona, Arizona.

Kate broke down in tears.

Regaining her composure, she sighed audibly and unconsciously ran a finger over the lettering on the card.

"God, I know that if You want me to go to this wedding, You'll make the way."

The statement was matter-of-fact because Kate was strong in her faith. In her daily chats with her Creator, she always spoke in a conversational tone. She believed God listened not only to her *prayers*—and answered them, according to His will—but also to her heart. She knew that *He* knew how desperately she wanted to be at that wedding! He also knew she was flat broke!

With only a part-time job and piles of medical bills, there was no way on earth she could afford a plane ticket from Melbourne, Florida, to Arizona.

Her recent phone conversation with Dana and James had been sad. Aware of her situation, the bride and groom wanted her to know the invitation was going out. They knew she'd been praying and praying for God to provide a way for her to attend. They truly wished they were in a financial position to be able to get her there, but that wasn't an option. No one had a solution.

All three of them cried.

For several years Kate had been dealing with some serious health issues. First, an auto accident left her with a fractured back. Then she was diagnosed with breast cancer and underwent a double mastectomy. After that, a heart disorder that had lingered since childhood required open-heart surgery. Next was the grim discovery that she'd suffered a stroke.

During this time the company she worked for collapsed and her mortgage underwriter job disappeared. Managers at a second mortgage company had no patience with her health problems, so she lost that job and couldn't find other work.

Yet Kate stood by God because she knew that He stood by her.

Her faith was tested, yet she refused to let any of these circumstances rob her of her joy. She maintained her upbeat personality and kept her vow to make at least one person smile every day.

Kate felt blessed the day she went for a job interview with Jeanne Ford, a manager at Cracker Barrel in Viera, Florida, a half hour from Kate's home. Jeanne was encouraging. Even though Kate did not try to hide her health issues—not even the scars on her chest from heart surgery—Jeanne said, "I love your bubbly personality. I don't have a lot of work, but we could try you out part-time."

When a server's position turned out to be too hard on Kate physically, Jeanne suggested she might be better suited to work as a cashier.

Kate thanked God profusely.

Again and again Jeanne saw the wisdom of the decision

to have Kate work as a cashier. But what Jeanne didn't know was that she herself was a Godwink Link. (That's the term I've coined for someone who delivers another person a Godwink without even knowing they're doing it.) Jeanne had no idea that her decision to hire Kate when others wouldn't would set the stage for Kate to experience the biggest Godwink of her life.

Kate was thrilled to get the part-time job as a cashier. It didn't completely cover her needs, but she would keep praying for another part-time job to cover her shortfall.

As Kate prayed and waited, Cracker Barrel treated her well, and her coworkers felt like family. So she always arrived a half hour before her shift to deliver cookies or just spread a little joy. And her job as a cashier continues to be a great fit.

"I love my job," exclaims Kate, "because I love talking to people!"

We can all learn from Kate. When, like Kate, we greet each day with an attitude of gratitude for the things God has given us, rather than donning a cloak of dark resentment for the burdens we must bear, He lets others see the joy in our hearts as He shines through us. Some will see—but not necessarily recognize—God's love in our warm smiles and welcoming ways. A few people will know the true Source of Kate's thankful spirit and ours.

As the day of the wedding grew closer, Kate faithfully *prayed* her intentional daily prayer just a teeny bit louder: "God, I know that if You want me to go to this wedding, You'll make the way!"

When the week of the wedding came, Jeannie considerately saw to it that Kate's schedule required more work hours than usual to help her keep her mind off the big event.

When Kate looked over the schedule, she appreciated that it called for her to work on Saturday, the day of the wedding, as well as the evening before.

So on Friday Kate arrived for work at three thirty, greeted her colleagues, put on her uniform, and, promptly at four, took her place behind the register.

It was a typical Cracker Barrel dinner crowd. The restaurant was jammed between five and six, and Kate chatted with everyone as they left, asking if they'd enjoyed themselves and cheerfully inviting them to "please come again."

"Kate, what in the world are you doing here! You should be at your son's wedding!"

It was Rose, one of Kate's coworkers, as she walked past the cashier's station. Kate knew Rose had been out of the loop, because pretty much everyone else had known for weeks that she would be missing the wedding.

"Well . . . I was feeling pretty good . . . till you mentioned it," Kate replied with the best smile she could muster.

She turned to see a man and a woman next in line ready

to pay their check. They both wore airline uniforms. Eager to change the subject, Kate smiled and said brightly, "Southwest! My favorite airline!"

The flight attendants smiled.

"You're missing your son's wedding?" inquired the woman, who had obviously overheard the exchange with Rose.

"Oh, yeah . . . I can't afford to go. He's getting married tomorrow north of Phoenix."

Not wanting to sound like she was feeling sorry for herself, Kate turned on her most cheerful attitude. "Hey, do you two fly to Vegas?"

"Yes," they both answered. "That's our regular route."

"Well, why don't you sneak me onto the plane, strap a parachute on my back, and shove me out over Phoenix!" Kate giggled.

Everyone laughed.

The airline workers paid their bill and said good-bye.

Kate continued ringing up customers.

Moments later she looked up and was surprised to see that the airline workers had returned. Both wore wide smiles. The woman glanced at Kate's name tag and spoke first.

"Kate, I'm Angela Gibbs. This is my fiancé, Ruben Darancou."

"Can you get tomorrow off?" asked Ruben.

"What?" said Kate, startled.

"We found two Southwest Buddy Passes in our bags in the car. Those are standby tickets to get you to Phoenix and back," Ruben continued.

Kate was dumbfounded. Her eyes began to fill with tears.

"Oh my! Thank you—and thank You, God!" said Kate as she put everything together and realized what was happening.

"She sure *can* get tomorrow off!" shouted Katrina, a co-worker who was at the register next to Kate's. "I'll take her shift!"

I don't believe this! thought Kate as her oft-uttered *prayer* flashed like a neon sign in her mind: *God, I know that if You want me to go to this wedding, You'll make the way.*

"Well, then, let's see how we can get you there," said Angie, pulling out her cell phone.

"What time is the wedding?" asked Ruben.

Wow, God! You really did it! said Kate inside her head. "Oh . . . uh . . . the wedding's at four p.m."

"OK, can you be at Orlando Airport for a six fifteen a.m. flight?" continued Angie, looking at the schedule on her phone. "That would get you to Phoenix at about eleven in the morning."

"Sure," said Kate, dazed by what was unfolding.

A small group was now gathering around her, all smiling joyfully. Everyone was feeling the excitement.

Before they left the restaurant, Angie handed Kate a business card with her number on it.

"Let us know how you make out," Angie said, smiling sweetly.

A short while later Kate was in her car, driving home to pack, grab about an hour's sleep, and then get up for the one-hour drive to Orlando Airport.

During the drive she kept repeating aloud, in disbelief, "Wow, God! You did it! You really did it!"

Later on, when she had time to reflect, she would clearly see that first Jeanne and then Angie and Ruben were all Godwink Links. Each of them was an unwitting player in a drama that became Kate's best Godwink ever! This experience reaffirmed for her that prayer works . . . and that when you are faithful to God every day of your life, when you remain in conversation with Him, He is right there beside you and faithful to *you*!

When Kate landed in Phoenix, she found her way to a bus to Sedona, learned the drive would take two hours, and was soon on her way. By the time she was close to her destination, Kate had made friends with the woman sitting next to her. Kate's excitement was visible.

"I can't wait to surprise everyone!" said Kate, beaming. "No one knows I'm coming. But I have a sense from God that when I walk into that hotel lobby, I'm going to see my eleven-year-old grandson running around." She laughed and added, "Most of my grandchildren call me Grammie, but Ethin made up a new name. I called him 'Pumpkin' one time, so he decided to call me 'Cupcake.'" She laughed again.

About two p.m. Kate walked through the front door of the hotel.

"Cupcake! What are you doing here?"

It was Ethin, just about to get on the elevator.

God was winking again.

The boy ran to Kate and hugged her.

She put a finger to her lips. "Shh. I want to surprise everyone. I need your help. Where's your mom?"

"She's in the beauty salon with Dana . . . and Uncle Jamie's upstairs. They have to get pictures taken."

"Then let's get busy," said Kate, lifting an eyebrow and smiling at her co-conspirator as she nudged him toward the front desk. There she shared her secret with the attendant, asking if she would call up to her son, James Kramer, and tell him there was a time-sensitive package for him in the front lobby that he had to come down right away and sign for.

James was feeling a bit annoyed. He had to finish getting dressed, he needed to be at a particular place for the bridal party photo shoot at a particular time, and now the front desk was insisting that he go downstairs right away for a "time-sensitive" package.

What the heck could be so time-sensitive? he kept asking himself as he rode down the elevator.

When the elevator doors opened, there she was! His mother!

"Wha— Wow—Mom! What are you doing here?" he blurted with a huge smile.

He took her in his arms and gave her a bear hug.

"Mom, you've got to tell me how you pulled this off! But not right now! Later! I've *got* to get to the photo shoot."

"All right! You go, honey," said Kate with a kiss. "We'll talk later."

She couldn't help giggling. This was definitely the best surprise ever!

A few minutes later Kate walked into the beauty salon and saw that Dana, the bride-to-be and her future daughter-in-law, and her daughter, Michelle, were standing at the register settling the bill. They were turned away from her.

"You two look beautiful. Are you attending a wedding?" asked Kate cheerfully.

"Mom!" said Michelle.

"Oh my God!" squealed Dana. "You made it!"

"Oh, Mom, this is so typical of you," added Michelle, grinning.

The three women air-kissed—they didn't want to mess up the makeup!—and said they couldn't wait to hear the whole story. Right now, though, Dana and Michelle were late for the photo session.

It turned out to be a beautiful wedding.

The next day, before heading back home, Kate had her heart warmed again. She had a long-harbored mother's concern that her son was not yet strong in his faith, but what she saw brought her to tears.

James had posted a touching statement on his Facebook page:

> My wedding day was just made perfect. My Mom surprised
> me as I knew she couldn't afford to come. I would love
> to thank the flight attendants that gave her a round trip
> ticket . . . they have, along with my new bride, strengthened
> my belief in God.

Upon arriving back in Melbourne, Kate couldn't wait to call Angie and Ruben to thank them again and provide the full wedding report that she'd promised.

Angie was excited and wanted to hear every detail. Then she asked a question.

"Kate, do you know of anyone who could help out Ruben and me? We have two children, and we fly three days at a time. Do you know of anyone who could be our nanny?"

Kate blinked. Could this be the other part-time job she had been *praying* for? Another Godwink?

"Uh, yes! *I* could be your nanny!" said Kate.

Once again she was amazed. *Wow, God! You sure* do *answer prayers, don't You!*

Louise and I have observed that Godwinks happen more often when you step out in faith and interact with others.

When you were a child, your parents no doubt told you, "Don't talk to strangers."

As adults, however, the very act of talking to a stranger sometimes opens the floodgate for Godwinks.

When you engage other people in conversation, as Kate did, you often position yourself for God to accomplish His purposes. As you saw, He put two strangers in Kate's path—Angie and Ruben—who became Godwink Links to answers to her *prayers.*

A primary takeaway from Kate's story is the power of *intentional prayer* to produce subsequent Godwinks and answered prayer. Daily, Kate prayed a specific request to God.

He heard, He listened, He delivered, as the Godwinks testify:

- Largely because of her upbeat personality, Kate got her first job, not in the mortgage field, but at Cracker Barrel.
- Kate prayed daily—and intentionally—for God to "make the way" for her to go to her son's wedding if God wanted her to go.
- Two kind-hearted flight attendants, Angie and Ruben, "just happened" to be in the cashier line as coworker Rose "just happened" to ask why Kate was not attending the wedding.
- Angie and Ruben "just happened" to discover unused standby tickets that they could give to Kate.
- And Angie "just happened" to need a nanny, giving Kate an answer to her prayer for a second part-time job.

On other occasions your prayer may be *unintentional*, almost a casual conversation with God. Ted's heartrending story below proves that, whether *prayers* are intentional or unintentional, God is paying attention.

~~~

Ted Harris's Christmas Blues Turn to Joy

It was an hour before dawn and still dark.

Unable to sleep, Ted strained to sit up in bed, struggling with the familiar heaviness of the unbearable, inescapable, unrelenting sadness that had weighed him down for one year to the day.

Prior to this day a year ago, Ted could at least cling to a thin thread of hope.

Then . . . the thread snapped.

How he hated to have to make that decision, to have to put his "precious angel" Kathy under hospice care on the eve of her favorite holiday, Christmas.

Am I calling for assistance too early? he wondered at the time, questioning the apparent insensitivity of the timing. *Will the children forever remember their mother's special holiday as the time Dad called in hospice?*

But what choice did he have? The ravages of ovarian cancer had claimed Kathy's body. Every doctor and every adviser said there were no more options, there was no hope. And though she was close to dying, no one could have known that she was so close to the end.

Still, did I do all that I could?

Then, in the morning darkness, Ted remembered the friend he had encountered at a store, a man who had lost his wife to cancer. The man looked seriously at Ted and said, "Don't do what I did. I waited too long to put my wife into hospice."

That's when Ted knew he needed to have help.

God, don't let me get in Your way, he had *prayed* silently.

Hospice had been wonderful. He recalled how skilled professionals responded quickly with a hospital bed and pharmaceutical supplies. They didn't immediately assign a hospice attendant but instead patiently guided him through this uncharted experience, providing him with careful instructions on how to medicate Kathy as needed.

Ted shuddered as he replayed the prior Christmas Eve in his mind.

Kathy had begun to cry out. The new medication was making her delirious, and she kept trying to get out of bed. Finally, after what seemed like hours, her eyes closed. But then Ted began to worry that perhaps she had gone into a coma. He was tormented, wondering if she would wake up. *What if I didn't get to say good-bye?* he thought, and a lump formed in his throat so big that it hurt.

Distraught, Ted placed his head in his hands. Soon he succumbed to pure exhaustion and slept on the floor for a few hours.

When he awoke on Christmas morning, Kathy was sitting up in bed!

"Morning, honey!"

She was alert! More alert than she had been in weeks!

"Do you have those books I bought for the boys?" she said, referring to two of their grandchildren.

"Yes, of course," said Ted, puzzled by her odd-but-welcome turnaround. He got the books right away. They were identical copies of *The Night before Christmas*. By clicking a button, she could read the story aloud and record it so the child could play it back over and over again. In clear diction Kathy read each book all the way through. Ted was astonished by her stamina.

As he wrapped the books in bright red paper, he couldn't help but think, given the circumstances, what a treasure these books would be for those boys. Long into the future they would be able to hear the classic Christmas tale told in their grandmother's gentle voice.

Later that day, Christmas afternoon, Kathy weakened. This time, she slipped into a coma from which she never returned.

The first anniversary of the loss of a loved one is always a mighty test of faith. As much as you'd like to avoid it, that date creeps toward you like an ominous dark cloud before a storm. You hope it'll just pass on by—quickly.

Ted put on his robe and walked into the den, illuminated only by the lights on the tree.

Before going to bed, he had finished the decorating, trying to put everything into exactly the place where Kathy would have wanted them. She was known for decorating to the hilt. There was hardly a spot—inside or outside the house—that didn't celebrate the birthday of Jesus.

Ted hung the stockings over the fireplace, draped the garlands here and there, and, very carefully—as she always reminded him—threaded the special family ornaments onto sturdy branches, making certain they were secure.

Now, in the slight chill of morning, he dropped into a chair and reassessed his decorating accomplishments in the dim, multicolored light from the tree.

As Ted studied the decor, he couldn't help but smile at the memory of Kathy's holiday exuberance. At this time of year, she was like a grown-up kid.

As if he were pulling the snapshots from a mental album, he pictured her Christmas ritual of handing out personalized ornaments to Ted and each of the children. Those ornaments had now multiplied to two or three dozen. Each had a prominent place on the tree, except for the ornament she gave to Ted one season—the little ceramic picture frame that sat on the table beside his chair. Kathy was afraid the frame might be a little too heavy to hang on the tree, so she always set it on the side table next to a Christmas candle.

As Ted gazed upon the ornament, his eyes started to moisten.

Inside the frame was Kathy's smiling face—just the way literally everyone remembered her. Kathy always smiled. Her photo was flanked by ceramic red-and-white candy canes, and across the top of the frame were the words *Merry Christmas*.

Oh, how Ted missed her.

God, please help me get through this holiday.

Ted knew that if he pushed that little button at the top of the picture frame, it would play a recorded message. He recalled that you had to press it with a fingernail, just right, to get it to work.

But he couldn't bear to do that. He couldn't bear to hear Kathy's voice. He had teared up the first time he heard it—and every year since. He knew that if he pushed that button now, he would cry like a baby.

Oh, God . . . if only she were here . . .

Forcing his thoughts in another direction, Ted determined it was still too dark in the room. Kathy always said that candlelight warmed up a room, so he pulled himself from the chair, went to the fireplace, picked up the lighter, and flicked the flame to light the candles on the mantel. Returning to his chair, he flicked the lighter again to ignite the candle on the side table, next to Kathy's picture.

Suddenly he was jolted. It was as if an electric shock had run through him. Kathy's voice was coming from the picture frame!

"Wha . . . ?"

Ted's mind searched for an explanation. *I didn't touch that frame. All I did was light the candle next to it!*

Again he flicked the lighter to ignite the candle, and again the voice of his dear wife came from the picture frame, mysteriously filling the quiet of the room!

Ted fell into the chair. And cried.

A few minutes later, he tried to sort it out. As a high school teacher and coach, he knew there must be a scientific reason for that phenomenon. Yet there was no accounting for the amazing timing—the divine alignment of his receiving this remarkable Godwink connection to his "precious angel" just when he needed it most. And just after he had said to God, in an *unintentional* prayer, "If only she were here."

A peace that surpassed all understanding began to flow over Ted. He knew that this was a Christmas Godwink he would never forget. He knew that God—and possibly his "angel" from heaven, Kathy herself—was sending a person-to-person link of joy to lift his spirits.

So, one more time, Ted flicked the lighter. This time giving it his full attention as Kathy's sweet voice filled the room:

"Merry Christmas, honey. I love you very much. Happy New Year."

Ted smiled. Almost giddy with joy, he flicked the lighter close to the frame again and again.

"Merry Christmas to you too, my darling wife. I'll see you in eternity . . . and I'll love you forever and ever."

Ted Harris believes that, although his *prayers* that morning were unintentional—he wasn't on his knees with folded hands, intentionally speaking to God—he was nonetheless in a state of *prayer* that had carried him through many days of grief.

Ted often chatted intentionally and directly with God, and Ted had definitely felt God's presence, right there by his side and Kathy's, during her last days this side of eternity.

AFTERTHOUGHT

God is always present with you. Even if you may not be speaking directly to God, He loves you so much that He feels your every hurt and knows every tear you shed. He looks at your loss, disappointment, conflict, and sorrow with compassion and love. So even if you don't intentionally *pray* to Him, God knows what kind of comfort you need exactly when you need it.

You keep track of all my sorrows.
You have collected all my tears in your bottle.
You have recorded each one in your book.
—PSALM 56:8 NLT

THE REST OF THE STORY

A year and a half after Kathy graduated to heaven, Ted was still visibly grieving his loss. Old friends who lived near Fort Worth, Texas, were prompted to throw a party for him. Ted felt he had no choice but to go, so he drove up from Houston to attend.

As he entered their home, he saw the banner.

It said, "Give Ted a Hug Party."

One of the people who had been invited was Jan McNeill, one of Ted's classmates at Texas Christian University forty years before. Their conversation rekindled fond memories.

Jan had been quite content with her single status for twenty-two years, but Ted's warm personality and sense of humor reminded her of years gone by. They began to date, and six months later they were married and began new chapters in each of their lives.

PRAYER THAT IS UNINTENTIONAL . . . AND EVEN UNASKED

We've seen how Kate spoke with God *intentionally* and how Ted spoke to Him *unintentionally*. But sometimes when you are overcome by the emotions of a situation, you find when you look back that you were *neither* intentional *nor* unintentional when you needed help. In fact, your request of God was actually *unasked*. Your *prayer* was not even prayed.

Still, God heard you.

That's what Patrick discovered.

Patrick and Margery: A Lost-Love Story

Patrick's eyes were drawn to the girl with the engaging smile and stylish outfit who was gliding across the dance floor with energy and grace.

He was the new kid in school, and this was his first seventh-grade dance.

"Who's she?" he asked the kid next to him.

Margery noticed the new guy staring at her. As she exited the dance floor, she "just happened" to end up right where he stood. Her smile was natural and sparkly.

They spoke, and a conversation began. Within days, everyone knew that Pat and Margery were an item.

Throughout high school Patrick Godfrey and Margery Southworth were a popular couple, attending most basketball and football games, class outings, and dances.

When high school came to an end, Margery approached the future with certainty: she selected a college in New Mexico where she would study biology.

Patrick was uncertain about his future. With no firm plan, he found himself lured to Hawaii to join a Tahitian band.

Life went on. And on. The two high school sweethearts drifted apart.

Margery became a career woman with Schick Safety Razor Company. She worked hard and felt accomplished. Still, she prayed that one day she would once again enjoy the kind of love she once felt with Pat.

Patrick made poor choices. He fell into two ill-conceived marriages, both ending in divorce. He concealed his hurts with alcohol, and as his life spiraled downward, his alcoholism intensified.

Fast-forward fourteen years.

Patrick very much wanted to rebuild his life, to leave behind his rudderless existence and start living with purpose. In order to raise his two young boys and gain some stability, he moved in with his mom in Palos Verdes, California, and got a job in Hollywood. He was sober and determined that his path would be straight.

One Sunday afternoon, he and his mother were looking through an old photo album. The pictures from high school brought back memories of a better time. When he turned the page to a shot of Margery Southworth and himself, his heart leapt. He missed her sweetness, her agreeable nature, and her sparkling smile.

"Why couldn't I have married Margery Southworth in the first place?" he said to his mother, shaking his head slightly.

Suddenly he had an overwhelming compulsion to find her. He asked his mother for the Los Angeles phone directory and began calling every "Southworth" listed. After numerous dead ends, he realized it was an impossible task. Margery couldn't be found easily. Perhaps she was married and had another name. Maybe she'd moved away.

He felt a deep sadness.

His mother said he was crazy.

"You should forget her. Just raise those two beautiful boys and forget about getting into another relationship for a while."

You could tell from the look on his mother's face that, as much as she would love to see her son happy and grounded again, she worried that finding Margery might only bring him more disappointment. She didn't want him to have yet another source of pain.

As he placed his head on the pillow that night, though, images of Margery's sweet smile flashed through his mind as he replayed his words from earlier in the day: *Why couldn't I have married Margery Southworth in the first place?*

Was Patrick *unintentionally praying* to find his high school sweetheart? Was he *asking* for God's assistance—for an answer to *prayer*, for a Godwink—without even realizing it? Maybe.

What we do know is that God was listening.

He always is.

The next morning Patrick began his daily one-hour commute to Hollywood. It was his custom to take the most direct route. But for some unknown reason, this morning Patrick had the unreasonable notion to take an alternate route, via Santa Monica. Knowing this would add thirty to forty minutes to his drive, he nevertheless went that direction. And he had no idea why he was doing so.

As Patrick pulled onto the long, two-lane ramp onto the 405 Freeway north, he slowed to a stop at the traffic light that managed the flow of cars onto the highway. He heard a beep.

He looked toward the van that was alongside him. He saw a beautiful woman with large sunglasses. Looking directly at him, she slowly lifted her sunglasses as if she were in a scene from a movie.

What? It was Margery! How could that be!

Patrick was shocked. How could this have possibly happened, less than twenty-four hours after he had received a sudden nudge to look for her? And when he was driving on a route he never took?

Overcome with emotion, he began to laugh . . . and then cry. Completely overwhelmed, he laid his head on the steering wheel in utter disbelief.

But he didn't stay in that position for long.

The cars behind him were beginning to honk. Soon there was a cacophony of horns as he looked again at the object of his dreams. Regretting that he had no choice, he proceeded up the on-ramp, soon to be immersed in the sea of cars on the freeway.

But he stayed to the right in case Margery could see him and so that he could pull off at the next exit. He put on his right-hand turn signal. He looked in the rearview mirror, and she responded by turning on hers!

He exited the freeway.

And so did she!

On the side street, Patrick and Margery chatted and laughed together for several minutes before both realized they needed to get to work. But Patrick was thrilled. Learning that Margery was not married, he had gotten her phone number and promised to call.

He couldn't wait to call his mother to tell her what happened. She whooped with glee. She loved Godwinks, and this one was unimaginable!

One week later Patrick and Margery went on their first date. All the joy and love of their high school romance was rekindled. They laughed and talked for hours, and once again they were an item.

One year later they were married and have lived happily ever after ever since.

Isn't God amazing? We find ourselves exclaiming, "How in the world did He do that?"

- At the time there were thirteen million people in the Greater Los Angeles Area and some four million highway vehicles.
- How could God cause two of those vehicles to be side by side on the same freeway ramp at the exact same moment?
- And how did He make it happen less than twenty-four

hours after Patrick was calling all the Southworths in the LA phone directory?

God is so tuned in to our lives that He listens even to our *unarticulated prayers*, and sometimes in response He delivers astonishing Godwinks.

AFTERTHOUGHT

Have you made bad choices and wondered if God could turn your life into something wonderful and worthwhile?

If you answered yes, you have a lot of company on this planet!

When he uttered those words, "Why couldn't I just have married Margery Southworth in the first place?" Patrick had no idea that God had a plan for turning his life around and making it something beautiful. Those words formed a *prayer*, an unintentional and unarticulated prayer. God heard Patrick's heart and swiftly went into action to divinely align him with his childhood sweetheart. What a Godwink!

God will never waste your pain. Only you can do that. God is in the salvage business, and He is just waiting for you to give Him your junk so He can turn it into treasure.

I consider that our present sufferings
are not worth comparing with the glory
that will be revealed in us.
—ROMANS 8:18 NIV

INTENTIONAL PARTNERED PRAYER™

For the past decade Louise and I have been champions of Partnered Prayer: of *praying* with another person on a regular basis.

To help people do that, we developed the 40-Day Prayer
Challenge™—a commitment to *pray* with someone for five
minutes a day for forty days.

In association with Baylor University's Institute for the
Studies of Religion, and some of America's biggest churches, we
ask people who sign up for the challenge to take a ten-minute
online survey on the first and fortieth days. This partnership
elevates the challenge from being a social experiment in Partnered Prayer to being the first empirical study of the outcome
of praying regularly with another person. Beta studies indicate
that Partnered Prayer with one's spouse may result in a 20 to
30 percent increase in conversation, respect, agreement, and
romance for couples and a drop in the fear of divorce to zero.
(More information can be found at www.40DayPray.com.)

Hugh and Joyce Pemberton decided to take the 40-Day Prayer Challenge. To put it another way, they entered into intentional Partnered Prayer for six weeks, and they were astonished to discover—as most people do—that *praying* consistently with another person expands the power of your prayer and divinely aligns your paths with Godwinks He wants to bless you with.

Hugh's Proof: The Power of Partnered Prayer

For Hugh and Joyce, life was good. Retired in Winter Haven, Florida, Hugh at seventy years old played golf four times a week. Their four kids were grown and on their own. The Pembertons had sold their successful business, and Hugh and Joyce had bountiful reasons—in their individual prayers—to thank God for blessings.

Then Hugh began having difficulty breathing. Why? What was going on? He had never smoked, he had led an active life, yet in October 2013 he was diagnosed with a lung ailment—interstitial pulmonary fibrosis—that can only be cured with a lung transplant. If that news weren't bad enough, the first two doctors he consulted said that, at age seventy-two, he was too old for the procedure!

Hugh's condition worsened, and he went on oxygen in October 2014. In the beginning he required three liters of oxygen per hour. Still, he maintained his faith and his fortitude, even dragging a small oxygen tank on wheels behind him wherever he went, including on the golf course.

More and more worry crept into Hugh and Joyce's private thoughts—more worry than they shared with friends or even with each other.

On a flight to visit her dying sister in Michigan, Joyce took a seat between a Navy veteran and his traveling companion. In conversation with the vet's companion, Joyce was astonished to learn that the woman's husband had the same lung diagnosis as Hugh!

Sitting in that particular seat turned out to be the first in a series of divinely aligned Godwinks. Joyce learned that the doctor who treated the woman's husband was the head of the Pulmonary Research Department at the famed Johns Hopkins Hospital in Maryland. Hugh and Joyce have a daughter in Maryland, so they arranged to visit her and, while they were there, get a second opinion on Hugh's condition from the doctor at Johns Hopkins.

Hugh and Joyce were ecstatic when the doctor gave him hope, assured him that he was *not* too old for a lung transplant, and told him the person to contact at the Tampa General Hospital's transplant program upon his return to Florida. And

Hugh did. After an interview with the team, he was scheduled for three days of testing and afterward was approved for the transplant list on December 5, 2015.

It came none too soon: Hugh's oxygen requirements had doubled to six liters per hour.

There was nothing left to do but *pray* and wait for a donor. The primary factors for matching a lung transplant donor to a recipient are compatible blood and tissue types and height. The heights of the donor and recipient need to be within two inches of each other.

Over the next four months, Hugh's hopes were raised twice . . . and dashed twice. Both times the news was that the donor criteria had not been met.

Hugh's health was now deteriorating rapidly. Joyce had to help him with everything. She clothed him, bathed him, and pushed his wheelchair. Whenever he moved from his bed to the wheelchair, he had to sit for fifteen minutes just to catch his breath. And his oxygen requirements rose to twenty liters per hour!

The situation didn't look good. When Hugh went on the transplant list, a pulmonary doctor at Tampa General told him that he had eighteen months to live, but based on the way he felt, Hugh was convinced he had considerably less time.

Hugh and Joyce continued to *pray* individually and, despite the difficulty, to regularly attend services at First Presbyterian in Haines City, Florida. At that church, the prayer teams in the congregation continued to pray for them.

On April 10, 2016, Louise and I spoke at First Presbyterian. We had been invited by our friend and former pastor Jeff Winter and his wife, Judy. Their personal story about the power of Partnered Prayer was featured in our book *The 40-Day Prayer Challenge*. In that story Jeff confessed that he was like the many busy pastors who prayed with their congregations on Sunday mornings and with their families at meals, but it hadn't crossed his mind to pray with Judy every day.

"I felt guilty," he said, upon recognizing the omission. "Although Judy and I had become one in the eyes of God when we were married, we were not becoming one in our spiritual life together. So I asked God to help me lay aside any matters of personal pride, and we accepted the 40-Day Prayer Challenge."

Jeff comments, "When we *pray* together as a couple, we are stripped bare emotionally. There is little room for pretense. I have discovered that as I listen to Judy and as we pray out loud, I hear her heart."

Jeff and Judy told of extraordinary results from the 40-Day Prayer Challenge, including an amazing return to faith by their son who had lost his way and become addicted to alcohol. Overnight Kyle turned his life around. Today he has a family and is serving as a missionary in Cambodia.

So Jeff and Judy wanted to share the power of Partnered

Prayer with their congregation in Haines City. For several weeks Jeff promoted our upcoming visit to the church as something people should not miss.

As arduous as it was, Joyce and Hugh got to church early that Sunday to claim one of the prime spots reserved for wheelchairs.

Upon hearing the convincing stories of how prayer becomes exponentially more effective when two people pray together, Hugh and Joyce immediately resolved to take the 40-Day Prayer Challenge. They committed to *pray* with each other for five minutes a day for forty days.

The next morning, April 11, they began. The five minutes were a little awkward at first, and they felt quite vulnerable. After all, Partnered Prayer is very intimate. They soon found themselves thinking that they needed to move from rote communication with God to a heart-to-heart conversation with Him. They also began *praying* for doctors to find a lung donor and for God to allow Hugh to live a long life so he could serve Him here on earth.

On April 13, Joyce felt a nudging, a sense that she was ill-prepared for upcoming events. The thought that the tires on their car might need to be replaced also crossed her mind, so she stopped at a tire shop.

"You shouldn't drive that car out of the driveway" was the

mechanic's grim assessment. He added that there was an hour-and-a-half wait to get the job done.

Because she was hosting a dinner party that night, Joyce told him she'd return on another day.

Yet, as she began to pull from the tire shop, Joyce felt another nudge. She realized that Tampa General Hospital was an hour and a half away and that the mechanic had just told her she shouldn't even leave the driveway.

She turned around and went back to wait. She would have the tires replaced right then. She got home almost two hours later, at five p.m.

When she went into the house, Hugh was on the phone. The Tampa General Hospital representative was telling Hugh that a lung donor had been identified and that he needed to get to the hospital as quickly as possible. If everything was in order, they would begin the surgical procedures at four the next morning, April fourteenth!

Within minutes Joyce canceled their dinner party, and they were on their way, thanking God for the impending answer to their prayer . . . and for the Godwink timing of four new tires to get them safely to the hospital!

And that's how Hugh and Joyce discovered for themselves how amazing the outcomes can be when two people *pray* together. Only three days after they began the 40-Day Prayer

Challenge, Hugh received his transplant. Two days later, though, he realized it was a bigger blessing than he'd thought. That was when he learned that, during surgery, the doctor had determined Hugh would receive two new lungs, not one! Wow!

Twelve weeks later Hugh was once again on the golf course, laughing with his buddies and playing his first game in months. God had given Hugh a second chance at life through a series of amazing Godwinks.

Let's look again at the ripples of the Godwink Effect.

Hugh and Joyce had received the devastating news that he needed a lung transplant to live but was too old to qualify. They *prayed*—individually—for positive resolution to this very dismal situation.

As we look back, we have to wonder . . .

- What if when Joyce boarded the plane, she had not been seated next to a Navy veteran whose traveling companion had a husband who suffered from the same medical condition as Hugh did?
- What if Joyce had been quiet that day rather than engaging the companion in conversation? She wouldn't have heard about Johns Hopkins Hospital's pulmonary program, information that prompted her to make an appointment with the doctor of the woman's husband, an appointment that gave Hugh and Joyce hope!

- Then, what if Jeff and Judy Winter had not taken the 40-Day Prayer Challenge? And what if they hadn't been passionate enough about their experience to want to share it with their congregation?
- What if Hugh and Joyce had continued to pray separately? What if they had not decided to take the challenge to elevate the power of prayer by praying together?

And after Hugh and Joyce had waited four months for a donor, isn't it just like God to provide them with an awesome answer to their Partnered Prayers only three days after they began the 40-Day Challenge? And then God answered their prayers with two lungs, not one!

We can go on and on. What if Joyce hadn't responded to those nudges from above to get the tires replaced? Would they have gotten to Tampa General in time for Hugh to be prepped for surgery?

The Godwink ripples on the lives of Hugh and Joyce are now much more obvious because, although we live our lives forward, we understand them backward. And we are wise to take the time to catalog God's favor in order to better appreciate the impact of our prayerful communications with Him.

ARE YOU ALLOWING GODWINKS?

A reader wrote this to us: *Godwinks happen when you allow them to happen.*

If we think about it, Godwinks are probably not likely to occur very often among people who refuse to allow God into their lives or refuse to acknowledge that He even exists, let alone believe that He is a benevolent presence in our lives.

But the situation is different for those of us who believe that we have been created by a God Who cares about us, Who allows us the free will to make our own choices even when those choices are unwise, unhealthy, or wrong, and Who forgives us for our errant ways when we simply confess those sins. We who believe in that manner are the ones who will begin to see Godwinks every day. And—as Louise and I have discovered—the more we converse with God through *prayer*, the more astonishing the Godwinks will be.

SECRET #2

ASK

A primary principle for experiencing answered prayer—for receiving Godwinks—is to ask. As revealed in the ancient Scriptures, "Ask and it will be given to you."

MATTHEW 7:7 NIV

TO ASK IS MORE POWERFUL THAN YOU THINK

I wonder if you had a grandmother like mine . . .

I was four years old as I stood gazing at the plate of chocolate chip cookies that were sitting on the kitchen table. Just out of the oven, they were still steaming, they had an unmistakably delicious smell, and they were just about at mouth level.

"Do you want one?" Mama Alice inquired in her British accent.

"I don't know," I answered weakly.

"Well, if you don't *ask*, you don't get," she said, as she pretended to go on with her work.

There was a pause as I decided to rearticulate my position.

"Yes . . . can I have a cookie?"

She smiled as she held the plate in front of me and watched me pick the biggest one.

That cookie was unbelievably delicious—and the lesson about the significance of the word *ask* was indelible.

It took a few more years before I figured out that Mama Alice was paraphrasing the ancient Scriptures: "You have not, because you *ask* not" (James 4:2 KJV, emphasis mine).

WHAT'S YOUR ASK?

I was speaking with a friend who worked in donor management. She was responsible for raising funds for a charity. I had just formed a nonprofit organization and was seeking counsel.

"What's your *ask*?" she inquired very directly.

The question put me on the defensive. I didn't know! I hadn't thought it out!

Not wanting to embarrass myself by admitting, "I don't know," I instead replied, "I was hoping you'd help us with that."

In her business—and perhaps in life in general—if you don't know what to ask, as Mama Alice counseled, you are not likely to get it.

The "ask" can be the amount of money you need to raise or the amount of money you wish to suggest that someone contribute. The "ask" is also designed to convince potential donors, in just a few words, why they should give to your cause.

Critical to successful fund-raising is a skillfully crafted "ask"—a simple sentence that you can speak with confidence and ease the moment you need it.

Whenever I need to fashion pitches for television series, book contracts, and a variety of other things, I combine what I learned from my "ask" experiences with my grandmother and the donor management lady.

In fact, whenever I need a new pitch, I always hear Mama Alice's voice saying, "If you don't *ask*, you don't get."

"ASK" IS AN IMPORTANT SECRET IN THE BIBLE

I have never doubted that my grandmother's lesson for me when I was a child was deeply rooted in the Holy Bible. She read that book every day. I'm sure she discovered that one of the earliest champions of the value of asking was none other than Jesus Himself.

Again and again Jesus told His disciples to *ask*. Below are about a third of the "ask" quotes found in the Bible, and I've emphasized *ask* so you don't miss it!

> *"If two of you on earth agree about anything they* ask *for,*
> *it will be done for them by my Father in heaven."*
> —MATTHEW 18:19 NIV

> *"Whatever you* ask *in prayer, believing, you will receive."*
> —MATTHEW 21:22 WEB

> *"If we* ask *anything according to his will, he hears us."*
> —I JOHN 5:14 NIV

> *"Whatever you* ask *in My name, that will I do,*
> *so that the Father may be glorified in the Son."*
> —JOHN 14:13 NASB

> "Ask *whatever you wish, and it will be done for you."*
> —JOHN 15:7 NIV

"If you ask *the Father for anything in My name,*
He will give it to you."
—JOHN 16:23 NASB

"All things for which you pray and ask,
believe that you have received them,
and they will be granted you."
—MARK 11:24 NASB

The simplicity of Jesus' teaching here is staggering. Christ's guidance to His followers is "Just *ask* in prayer." That's it. Just *ask.*

And asking is a secret to more Godwinks.

Mary and Fran: You Just Need to Ask

Mary's Simple Wisdom

Mary Pace was married to Antonio for fifty-seven years, and she raised their six children with simple guidelines. In her Brooklyn-Italian accent, she would say, "You just need to *ask.*"

For as long as she can remember, Mary wove similar principles from Scripture into her conversations, especially with her children. This lesson was "You have not, because you *ask* not" (James 4:2 KJV). And Mary believed it.

Consider this amazing story—and the amazing Godwink—from Mary and Tony's early years of marriage, when every dollar was dear and Mary hadn't yet learned to drive . . .

It was after supper, a beautiful evening, and they were in the backyard of their home on Long Island. They were within sixty miles of the Statue of Liberty, which had greeted them when they arrived from Italy. As Mary watched her husband weeding in the garden, she suddenly had an idea.

"Tony! Let's get in the car and go get an ice cream!"

Tony glanced up, his hands covered with dirt, shook his head, and said, "No, Mary. Not tonight."

"Come on, Tony! You'd like an ice cream!"

Antonio shook his head and continued working.

"Aw, Tony . . ." Gazing into the sky, Mary half-jokingly said, "I wish I had my own money and my own car. I'd drive myself to get an ice cream."

At that very moment something extraordinary happened—something that had no logical explanation. It was a Godwink so profound that it shaped and upheld Mary's belief system. From that time forward, whenever she said to her children—Frannie, Giacinta, and Antonietta—"You just have to *ask*," they always pictured in their minds what happened to their mother that evening in the backyard. You see, as Mary lifted up her eyes to the heavens, something was fluttering down.

She held out her two hands, and the gently floating object landed in them. It was a twenty-dollar bill!

How could that be?

Utterly astonished, Mary looked around. There was no nearby building, no person anywhere, and absolutely no evidence of where the bill had come from. All Mary knew was that she had indirectly *asked* God for something unnecessary and simply fun—money to buy an ice cream cone—and now she was holding a twenty-dollar bill!

God does things like that, and that's what Godwinks are often about. Remember the wink you got across the dining table, from that favorite relative, and how that wink communicated love, connection, and reassurance—*Hey, kid, I'm thinking about you right now*. Godwinks are like that. Godwinks are one way God stays in touch with you, providing encouragement, and answering prayers.

So a twenty-dollar bill floats out of nowhere. Stunned, Mary asks, "How could that happen?" And how could it happen just as she was wishing for ice cream money?

How?

God.

That's how it could happen!

Fran's Story: Just Ask

"Frannie, you just have to *ask*."

Her mother Mary's sweet voice had spoken those words to her since she was a toddler, and they were engraved in the mind of Fran Boyd.

Now a mother herself—she had two kids in college—Fran, at forty-seven, had many reasons to be grateful.

Her Christian faith had always been strong. God just seemed to be there every time she needed Him. Even on 9/11.

Twelve years earlier, she and Brian were living three blocks from the World Trade Center in New York. On the tragic morning she, Gloria, and Irene—two mothers from her kids' school—had dropped off the children, met in the schoolyard, and were heading out for coffee at a WTC café a couple of blocks away. But they were delayed. At the last minute, Gloria "just happened" to run into her friend Annie, whom she hadn't seen in fifteen years. For several minutes the two women stood chatting, catching up, and telling stories. And that encounter was most likely the reason Fran, Gloria, and Irene were not in the WTC coffee shop at the moment New Yorkers in southern Manhattan heard the unusual roar of a passenger plane flying extremely low.

Instinctively, Fran and the others ducked and then, bewildered, looked up. They were shocked as they saw a 767 slam into one of the world's tallest skyscrapers! The mothers instantly ran to gather their children from their classrooms.

On the way Fran speed-dialed Brian. Thank God the call went through. Brian was at his desk in a building close to the World Trade Center. Hearing her frantic words, he looked out the window and saw the WTC spewing smoke and a storm of white paper—like a strange ticker tape parade. But before Fran and Brian could make a plan to meet, the connection was lost.

Speaking over the intercom, a school administrator cautioned everyone to be calm and to stay where they were. Despite those instructions, Fran quickly led Sarah and Brian Jr. off campus. Accompanied by Gloria and her daughter, Fran and her two kids began running up the west side of Manhattan. Where they were heading, they didn't know—they just needed to get away!

Darting this way and that to avoid colliding with others who were running in the same direction, Fran began to lag behind. *Darn, why am I wearing platform sandals?* She thought of a moment from earlier in the day. As she was getting dressed, this question flashed across her mind: *Shouldn't I wear comfortable shoes today?* But she hadn't listened to the nudge.

"Mommy! Come on!" Six-year-old Brian was calling out to her. He had run several yards ahead.

In that instant, the crowds of worried people slowed as every single person turned and looked behind them. There was another roar, like the first one. A second plane was plowing into the second World Trade Center tower with billowing flames and smoke. The horrific image would be etched on their minds for years to come.

Fran's first thought: *The towers may fall. Right where we're standing!*

Fran prayed and asked God to keep her children safe, to keep Brian safe, and to help her and the kids get away despite the clumsiness of her shoes.

New Yorkers were unable to phone each other that September morning. Yet, strangely, spotty phone service *did* work to places outside the city. Fran's sister-in-law Karen lived in Michigan, and she became the point person, giving Fran peace of mind with the message that Brian was indeed safe. Karen also guided everyone to a rendezvous point: Gloria's mother's apartment in SoHo.

Once they were back in each other's arms, Fran and Brian concluded that they may have lost everything: Brian's technology job on Wall Street and possibly their home and all their possessions. But the ripple of miraculous Godwinks had kept their family together and safe.

Thank You, God.

Over the next few days, information came slowly. Fran and Brian learned that their apartment was off-limits, behind a chain-link fence, and under the watch of the National Guard, for an undetermined period of time.

For all intents and purposes, Fran and Brian's world was collapsing, but God had embraced them, He was with them, and He would raise them up.

By God's grace and out of the rubble of their circumstances, Fran and Brain reinvented themselves and started a thriving social media agency, now a leader among the world's largest faith-based organizations. Among the Media Connect Partners' clients today are Joel Osteen's Lakewood Church, pastor John Hagee, CBN's *700 Club*, and many more.

Fast-forward twelve years . . .

When Brian Jr. selected Tulsa as his destination for college, Fran and Brian decided to get an apartment there as well; after all, they could operate their social media company from anywhere. Sarah was also glad to be near her brother. Shortly after they moved, Fran was completely unprepared for the sledgehammer of fear and worry that crashed down upon her with the doctor's prognosis of her probable death—"You have cancer, and it's a very aggressive type."

She wanted to scream and challenge the doctor's report. After all, only a couple of weeks earlier she had been told that she had cancer that was *not* the aggressive type. The nurse had even said, "If you have to have cancer, this is the best kind to have."

She was shocked, confused, and even feeling punished by God, as the reality sank in. *I could really die!* Her mind began a wild search for answers: *This doesn't make sense. Me? With cancer?*

One month before, to the day, she had run across the finish line of her third marathon. There was no family history of cancer. And she followed a good diet.

And how could the doctors reverse the diagnosis like that? Or had they misread something? How could she now trust anything they told her?

Are you in this somewhere, God? Fran allowed herself to wonder. And almost immediately, like a comforting blanket, came her mother's simple words that she had heard so often when she was a child: "You just have to *ask*, Frannie."

God, will You help me, please? What should I do?

Run. She was a runner. That's what she always did when she needed to clear her mind.

She called her daughter, Sarah, to see if she would join her.

As mother and daughter ran, Fran began to explain the scary diagnosis to Sarah. But in her head, she again asked, *God, what should I do?*

Pausing for a red light, they ran in place on the sidewalk.

That's when Sarah looked up. The statement on a billboard above them seemed to be entering into their conversation.

"Mom, look!"

Fran read the sign: "The first step in fighting cancer? A second opinion." Below was the name of the billboard's sponsor: Cancer Treatment Centers of America.

Fran and Sarah looked at each other. When they resumed their run, each had a new thought rolling through their minds: *a second opinion.*

Upon hearing about the diagnosis, Fran's parents and sisters, Giacinta and Antonietta—still in New York—had also suggested getting a second opinion. "Come back here. We have the best doctors," they had said.

But Fran wanted to seek out her options in Tulsa first. She couldn't stop thinking about that billboard she had seen on her run. *Was that a sign from God? Was that God talking to me through a billboard? Could the Creator of the world do that for me?*

She called Brian and asked him to contact the Cancer Treatment Center Hospital in Tulsa to see if they took their family's medical insurance. Her heart sank when, a short while later, Brian called back and said, "No, they don't."

What should I do, God?

The doctor's death sentence again ran through her mind: "You have cancer, and it's a very aggressive type."

Fran sighed. She remembered something she'd seen on her calendar. She sighed again. The last thing she wanted to do that evening was go to a church event and listen to a speaker. But their friend Chadwick Mohan—pastor of a forty-thousand-member church in Chennai, India—was speaking at a modest-sized church in Tulsa, and Fran and Brian had promised him they would go.

Suck it up, she resolved. *You have to go.*

It turned out that Chadwick's message directly applied to Fran's state of mind. "Fear does not come from God," he said, telling the story of Shadrach, Meshach, and Abednego (see Daniel 3). "Even in the fire, God was with them."

Fran felt a calmness and peace flow over her. Somehow, she sensed, she was going to be OK.

After Chadwick's talk, Zack Varughese, the host church's senior pastor, sensed that two people wanted to speak with him. (It's a sense that pastors seem to develop after many years in the ministry, and Zack had served four decades.) Although he normally exited quickly from the Wednesday night service—because of an early-Thursday-morning obligation at his corporate desk—Zack approached the couple.

Fran and Brian were pleased to see the pastor walking toward them. For some reason, Brian felt they should meet him and talk with him. The man extended his hand and introduced himself. They chatted for a few moments.

At one point, though, Fran glanced sharply at her husband. He had just asked an odd, almost impertinent question to the man he had just met.

Later, Brian told Fran that something about Zack Varughese suggested that pastoring was not his only vocation. "He had the air of a successful businessman, not a preacher," he explained as they drove home.

It definitely took Fran by surprise to hear Brian unexpectedly *ask* the pastor, "Do you have a career in addition to pastoring?"

Zack smiled. In a measured manner he replied, "Yes. I work at Cancer Treatment Centers of America."

Did my eyes just widen like Brian's? wondered Fran.

"Really? What do you do there?" asked Brian.

"I'm the Senior Vice President of Oncology Services," said Zack, humbly.

Astonished, Brian paused to contemplate what the man had just said.

And Fran simply broke down sobbing.

Quickly trying to explain herself despite a sudden storm of tears and emotion, Fran blurted out jumbled thoughts in a cracking voice: "My doctor said I have the worst kind . . . The billboard told me about you . . . But you don't take my insurance."

She tried so hard to rein in her tears.

Brian calmly took over, explaining that the conflicting diagnoses had led Fran to consider the message she auspiciously saw on the CTCA billboard. Fran was convinced that it was a sign from above.

"God showed you one sign," said Zack, smiling, "and now you're looking at a second sign—this one from Cancer Treatment Centers. Can you come to my office tomorrow?"

Zack took out his phone, checked his calendar, and arranged a time for them to be at his hospital office the next day. "We'll look into your insurance and make sure you get a second opinion," he reassured them.

As they left the church, Fran and Brian discussed—in awe—the breathtaking size of the Godwinks they had experienced. First, in response to Fran's asking for God's help, was the nearly instant appearance of the CTCA billboard providing the guidance Fran wanted: "Get a second opinion." Then she fought a strong desire to stay home that evening despite their prior arrangement to see a friend from India speaking at a church. Then, when they were there, Fran and Brian "just happened" to meet the senior pastor who "just happened" to be a top executive for Cancer Treatment Centers of America!

Was there any doubt that God was in this series of events? He was absolutely right in the middle of all these Godwinks.

* * *

Cancer Treatment Centers of America runs some of the best hospitals in the country, and they are staffed by top physicians from all over the world. Fran felt an immediate warmth when she entered the building. She felt cared about as a patient, and the doctors and nurses treated her like a friend, not just a number.

At their initial meeting, Pastor Zack asked Brian when his insurance would expire, and Brian said, "In about a month." So Zack recommended they contact another insurance firm, one accepted by CTCA. They worked out all the issues, and Fran would get her second opinion. A plan was put into place just before Christmas. Fran had her surgery two weeks into the new year, and she left the hospital cancer-free. Nine months later she ran another marathon.

Fran and Brian can look back and clearly see the Godwink Effect in their life.

But what was the first pebble in the pond, causing every subsequent ripple? Maybe it was the very moment Fran's mother Mary learned those words from the ancient Scriptures:

> *Whatever you* ask *for in prayer,*
> *believe that you have received it,*
> *and it will be yours.*
> —MARK 11:24 NIV

Every time Mary subsequently said to Fran, "You just have to *ask*, Frannie," her daughter became stronger and more resolute in her own faith. Mary didn't need to speak with the sophistication of a preacher; she spoke with the simple faith of a child. And after all, isn't the faith of a child what God wants from all of us?

As children, we probably had the experience of throwing pebbles into a pond and seeing the ripple effect. Your prayer life works the same way. Each prayer is a pebble dropped into the pond of your life causing a spontaneous effect, resulting in successive Godwinks and answered prayers. The greater your faith, the greater the number of ripples on your pond of life.

Ask God to give you a childlike faith similar to Mary's simple "Just *ask*."

Try it! Be a pebble thrower!

ASK, SEEK, AND KNOCK

Another passage in Scripture provides an even bigger promise:

> Ask *and it will be given to you;*
> *seek and you will find;*
> *knock and the door will be opened to you.*
> —MATTHEW 7:7 NIV

Still, there are times in life when God seems far away. Very far away.

Have you experienced that kind of dark season and wondered if God had pushed the pause button on you?

When that happens, we need to make a conscious effort to remain focused on Him every day by praying, reading His Word, and holding on to His promises.

Eventually you will know His presence again. That's another promise:

> *He will not leave you nor forsake you.*
> —DEUTERONOMY 31:6 ESV

ASKING VIA INTERCESSORY PRAYER

Praying on behalf of another person is called intercessory prayer. When you ask for God to bless another person, you are inviting the power of prayer to impact that person. You are joining your prayers with their own prayers and the prayers of other intercessors.

This principle, which I think of as "mutual lift," is exemplified in the following story from Sonja Henry Harper.

~~~

Sonja and Randy: Help from the Prayer Garden

"C'mon, Wayne. Let's go to the garden," said Michele Mazzola Smith, holding her coffee mug and leading the way to their prayer garden. They walked into a sheltering of trees and flowering plants, with its statues and a water fountain, located near their home in Orange, Texas.

It was eight a.m.

Ever since they were married, Michele and Wayne have treasured this ritual of sitting on the stone bench, breathing in the fresh scent of morning, acknowledging the beauty of God's birdsong orchestrations, and beginning their daylong conversation with the Lord.

They had become known as prayer intercessors, and people found comfort in knowing that their concerns were being messengered directly to God from Michele and Wayne's cozy sanctuary.

"Good morning, Father," began Michele. "Today we *ask* for your blessings upon Sonja Henry . . ."

Sonja Henry, a dental hygienist, was sipping her morning coffee as she studied the schedule for the day.

It was eight a.m.

The name on the appointment schedule was Randy Harper. She didn't know him. He was handsome with an attractive gentlemanly quality about him.

Hmm . . . I wonder if Michele Mazzola Smith is praying for me in the prayer garden right now.

Flashback to twenty-four hours earlier . . .

"Hey, Sonja! I'm running behind. Can you take one of my patients?"

Sonja Henry had a break in her schedule.

"Sure," said Sonja, smiling at her coworker and glancing at the appointment lineup. She knew the name of the patient—Michele Mazzola Smith—but they'd never met.

Sonja introduced herself.

"Mrs. Smith, we have a Godwink: you were a patient of my former boss. And close friends, I believe." She named the practice.

"Why, yes. My husband and your boss were best of friends."

Sonja explained that everyone in the office had been terribly saddened when they heard that Michele's husband had passed away because of cancer.

"That's nice of you to remember from so long ago," said Michele. "But you know, God takes care of everything. He blessed me with a second godly man, a man who loves the Lord just as my first husband did."

"How wonderful! And that's exactly what I need," said Sonja. "I've been divorced for thirteen years and never had a godly man in my life."

As they chatted, Sonja confided that subsequent to her divorce, her "man-picker" had been ineffective. In fact, she said, a friend had just recently asked what kind of man she would like to meet.

"So I told her my secret wish list that I hadn't shared with anyone but God," said Sonja. "First, he has to be a believer. Second, I want a man who'll be my best friend: I want to be able to sit and have coffee together. I'd love it if he rode a Harley and had some experience in the military because my adoptive dad was in the military.

"Then my friend said, 'Don't forget to *ask* for a man who's hot!' But honestly, Michele, more important than that is what you have . . . a godly man."

Michele took Sonja's hand, looked at her tenderly, and said, "My dear, I believe we have had a divine appointment today. My husband, Wayne, and I have a prayer garden. Every morning we go to our garden and pray for people. Tomorrow morning at eight a.m., we are going to pray that God sends you a godly man."

Sonja smiled and squeezed Michele's hand as she whispered, "Thank you."

Now, just about twenty-four hours later, Sonja found herself looking into the kind eyes of Randy Harper.

Do You have something to do with this, God? she mentally inquired.

"So, does your wife come here as well?" *asked* Sonja gently.

Randy shook his head. "No, I'm divorced."

Oh my! Maybe You do, Lord!

Sonja's heart fluttered. "Oh, I understand. So am I. Divorced."

As they chatted, Randy's appointment seemed to last a little longer than usual.

Randy Harper had been divorced for a year, and he still felt the sting of the hurt. He had absolutely no intentions of getting involved in another relationship; he wasn't interested and he wasn't looking. To all well-meaning matchmakers he had said, "I am very comfortable being just with myself and God."

Yet, sitting in Sonja Henry's dental chair, he began to wonder, *If I'm so darned comfortable being by myself, why am I feeling this tugging inside?*

Then, almost against his resolve and outside his control, that inner tugging found its voice—and it was an awkward one. "Uh . . . would you like to go out to dinner sometime?"

Sonja blushed, and just as awkwardly as the question, she replied, "Well, it's not like I don't know you. I've had my hands in your mouth!"

They both laughed.

Sonja couldn't wait to call Michele Smith to find out whether she and Wayne had indeed been in their prayer garden, praying for her, at eight o'clock that morning, the very time Randy Harper was climbing into the dentistry chair.

And they had been!

Unquestionably, when Michele and Wayne *asked* God to send a godly man to Sonja, God listened!

Two days later Sonja and Randy had their first date. It was

on February thirteenth because Randy felt Valentine's Day might seem a bit clichéd. One year later, on the anniversary of that first date, Sonja and Randy were married.

Somewhere along the way, Sonja reviewed her wish list for a husband that she'd shared only with God, with her girlfriend, and with Michele Mazzola Smith. Sonja was able to check off every single wish: Randy is a godly gentleman, he rides a Harley, and he served in the military. And he is definitely her best friend, with whom she shares a cup of coffee every morning.

And yes, as mentioned earlier, he's hot!

POSTSCRIPT

When are you crossing the line with God and asking Him for too much?

Sonja wrestled with that issue after her divorce. She wanted to add another item to her wish list: she wanted to ask God for a man who shared her affection for Germany, her native country.

She thought about it but left it off the wish list she shared with Michele.

But proving that God listens not only to your words but

also your heart, she discovered that Randy's military service had sent him to Germany. He loved that country almost as much as Sonja did. Her joy soared.

When they were able to travel to Germany—to visit both the place of Sonja's childhood and the base where Randy had been stationed—the time was a treasure.

So, back to the question above, "When are you asking God for too much?"

Never. He wants to hear about everything that's on your heart.

If for some reason your current wish is not His will—because He has a different, even better plan for you—He provides perfect peace as you trust in Him.

A Thought about Soul Mates

Webster's dictionary defines *soul mate* as "a person who is perfectly suited to another in temperament."

We all want to find that kind of partner, don't we? Life's journey is so much sweeter when we have someone to share it with. Deep down inside, each of us wants a companion who will be by our side, and watch our back, in every situation.

But we wonder, *Is there a perfect person out there for me?*

If so, where do I look?

And how will I know if I've found the right one?

The best way to deal with those questions is to ask God for guidance. After all, Scriptures say to acknowledge Him in all your ways, and He will direct your steps (Proverbs 3:6). Also ask God to give you patience and peace as you trust that He is working to divinely align you with the perfect soul mate.

BELIEVE

---

*Faith is critical to having our prayers
answered, to seeing Godwinks. Faith comes
from* believing *that God is who He says He is
and that He can do what He says He can do.*

LET'S TALK ABOUT FAITH

You may remember, as a child, standing on a dock or the side
of a swimming pool and looking at your father's outstretched
arms as he said, "C'mon! Jump!"

And you did. You didn't hesitate. You'd done it before, and
you had complete faith that your dad would catch you. He
always did.

71

Similarly, as you waited for your mom to pick you up after school or from a friend's house, you rarely worried. You had faith that she'd be there just like she said she would.

Your faith in God matures and grows stronger the same way: the more you let yourself fall into His arms—the more you trust that He'll catch you, rescue you from danger, get you out of tough jams, or help you achieve a goal—the more you'll find that He has caught you once again. The more strongly you *believe*, the more He'll catch you.

And that's the place you want to be in your walk with God—*believing*.

When you *believe* that He is who He says He is . . . and that He can do what He says He can do, then you're applying Secret #3 in order to experience more Godwinks and answered prayer.

When doubts about God are no longer part of your thinking, then you will be at the same place in your faith to which Tim Jones arrived.

His Godwinks—and the Godwinks of his new friend Don—were extraordinary.

~~~

Tim and Don's Amazing Mercy Mission

Just after sunrise on a Saturday morning in October, things were beginning to stir in Kannapolis, a small city a half hour north of Charlotte, North Carolina.

Pastor Tim Jones was moving through the church campus, putting things in place for the Craft and Bake Sale. Mercy Independent Church was just two months old, and today's open house would introduce the new facility to the community.

As he set up the "Meet the Pastor" table near the front door, Tim plugged in his audio system and aimed the loudspeakers into the front yard and parking lot. For a moment he wondered if this would be a significant day for his new church and his family.

In another part of Kannapolis, Don Herbert was up early. He remembered that Belinda wanted to stop by the Craft and Bake Sale at that new church. She loved poking around those kinds of events. He'd be fine—he always was—just waiting in the car, studying lyrics to some new songs. Don enjoyed singing with a gospel group in his spare time.

Tim lifted his favorite Gaither Vocal Band CD from the case, selecting repeat on the playback so it would play again and again over the loudspeakers. His favorite song—"Sow Mercy"—was on that CD. As he tested the song on the sound system, one of the lyric lines tugged at his memory: "Grandma's got a secret you should know."

He remembered the first time he heard that phrase, thinking, *I have a secret too. No one knows about the torture and abuse I suffered as a child at the hands of six different stepfathers. I am alive today only by the grace of God.*

Yet "Sow Mercy," he realized, is not about secrets like his. The song, by writers Reba Rambo-McGuire and Dony McGuire, is about sowing God's grace in the lives of other people. The chorus offers listeners this important reminder:

> *You always reap exactly what you sow.*
> *Sow mercy.*
> *Sow grace.*
> *Sow kindness*
> *Sow faith.*

Catching himself lost in thought, Tim dismissed his musings and got busy on the task at hand: preparing for the first event at his new church.

Driving to the church, Don knew Belinda liked to get to yard sales and craft shows early, before everything was picked over.

"I'll see you in a little bit," said Don, as he pulled into a parking spot next to the church. As Belinda got out, he put the windows down so he could smell the fall air.

As he enjoyed the colorful autumn scene, he remembered that he had another critical doctor's appointment in just a week or so. A twinge of anxiety broke through his usual barriers. He promptly forced himself to think about something else. Then he heard it—the music wafting from the church. He perked up. It was "Sow Mercy," his favorite song.

As a gospel singer, Don had long loved the Gaither Vocal Band and admired the moving lyrics.

Don got out of the car and headed toward the music. There, Pastor Tim greeted Don with a handshake, asked a few friendly questions, and told him about the new church.

"You're playing one of my favorite gospel bands," said Don, "and I love 'Sow Mercy.'"

"That's my favorite too," said Tim, leading Don into the building for a tour.

The two men had no idea that an incredible Godwink had just occurred—nor could either have imagined the many Godwinks that were about to unfold.

Having learned during their chat that Don was a singer, Tim asked if he and his group would be willing to appear at a church event in November.

Don smiled wholeheartedly and said, "Sure!"

Strangers only minutes before, the two traded contact information and went on their ways.

In the car Don was beaming as he told Belinda what happened. "I thought I was walking into a yard sale so I could hear my favorite song, and I walked out with a gig!"

Several days later, however, neither Don nor Belinda was smiling as they left the doctor's appointment at Duke University Hospital. They walked with a heaviness, their hearts broken and dreams dashed. The news they had received was nothing short of tragic. Don's life was in peril.

The liver transplant he'd had six months earlier was causing his kidneys to fail. Now he needed a kidney transplant—and he needed it immediately. The medical tests had shown that Don also had a life-threatening heart blockage, but until they could replace his kidney, they couldn't risk doing the heart surgery. The final blow, sinking their hopes even further, was the news that finding a kidney donor was a one-in-twenty-thousand chance, and it could take five to seven years.

The situation seemed totally hopeless.

Even when they were back at home, Don looked shell-shocked. Belinda took his hands into hers and gazed into his eyes. With authority she said, "Let's pray."

Belinda prayed for a long time. Interrupted by bursts of tears, she begged God, pleaded with Him, and finally threw herself at His feet.

"God, we have no other choice. We have to *believe* in You. And with You, there are no impossible situations!"

The kidney donor Don and Belinda were praying for had to have the same blood type as Don's and be a nonsmoker. But they also needed to satisfy a checklist of twenty additional health requisites. Over the next few days Don and Belinda learned that none of their family members or friends were qualified to donate a kidney.

Belinda continued to cry and to pray.

The thought entered her mind that they needed to use every possible tool to find a donor, and one far-reaching tool is social media. She went to her computer and poured out her heart on Facebook.

"It is so hard to ask, and so humbling, but I want the man I love to live a long life. I want to grow old with him, by my side."

Her painful appeal went on the wings of angels into the Internet, fueled by Belinda's and Don's prayers. "God, we *believe* You when You say, 'If you don't ask, you don't receive.'"[1]

---

1 CBN, *700 Club*, http://www.cbn.com/700club/features/amazing/SW227_don_herbert _and_tim_jones.aspx.

*   *   *

The first man to read Belinda's plea choked up as her words pierced his heart. It was Tim Jones! He immediately spoke with his wife, Sherry, and she knew her husband well enough to know that this was a call he had to make.

Tim picked up the phone and called Belinda.

"I know I only met your husband that one time, and I'm not calling to be a hero," said Tim. "But I would like to help you in some way, including even possibly seeing if I can qualify as a donor."

The two couples agreed to meet that evening.

Tim and Sherry talked about it and prayed.

"God has been so good to us, Sherry. I just feel that I need to be obedient to Him. Look what God's done for us. My childhood was a daily prison of hopelessness, pain, and shame. Yet He lifted me out of that bondage, and He led me to you—my wonderful wife—and He's given us a blessed life."

Tim felt there was great significance in what he was considering. He had personally experienced God's amazing grace. Now he felt God was telling him to see if he could be a donor, and Tim wanted to obey. He also thought about the scriptural message of the song, "Sow Mercy," that had mysteriously aligned the two men:

Let's till the soil and pull some weeds
And here's your bag of precious seeds . . .
You always reap exactly what you sow.

When the two couples met that evening, they talked and prayed together. At the end of the evening Tim said, "I've decided to see if I can be your donor."

After days of arduous testing and a few weeks of waiting, Tim received a letter from Duke University Hospital. What it said surprised him: "You are a perfect match!"

The two couples were elated. Tim was the one in twenty thousand.

It was four and a half months from the time Tim and Don first met, on that Saturday in October, to the day of the surgery.

After having dinner together the previous evening, the four of them arrived at Duke University Hospital at dawn. Doctors explained that Tim would be taken into surgery first to have a kidney removed. Then, approximately two hours later, Don would go into surgery for the transplant.

Don, Belinda, and Sherry waited together. The two hours seemed to go by slowly with no news from the operating room.

Then the third hour. The fourth, the fifth, and the sixth hours! The three of them were getting worried. Very worried.

What could be going on? Why was the procedure taking so long? they each wondered.

After seven hours in the operating room, the surgeon came out, and nurses quickly began to prep Don for his surgery.

"We had an unusual situation," explained the surgeon. "Everything was going according to schedule, but then we discovered something that hadn't shown up in any of Tim's testing. Behind the kidney we removed, we discovered an aneurysm on his renal artery. I know that's startling, but it was good we found it. If we hadn't, chances are it would have ruptured, and those events are nearly always fatal."

Later, looking directly at Tim, the doctor said, "Today you saved Don's life, Tim. In so doing, you saved your own."

Tim Jones and Don Herbert are now like brothers. They often appear together on television or at speaking engagements: Tim tells the story and preaches; Don sings.

They share the message—and remind themselves—that our powerful God Almighty can astonish us with answered prayers and Godwinks more amazing than we could ever imagine.

The Godwinks that Tim and Don encountered were uncanny:

- They were drawn together at Mercy Independent Church by their mutual love of the song "Sow Mercy."
- The odds of finding a kidney donor are one in twenty

thousand. It's truly an extraordinary Godwink that Tim was a perfect match for Don.

- Then, for doctors to find the aneurysm—that ticking time bomb inside Tim's body—only because they removed a kidney, is mind-boggling. What if they had chosen to remove the *other* kidney?

- Finally, there's this sweet and very fitting Godwink in the McGuires' "Sow Mercy" lyrics:

If you ever reached to help a friend
A hand you held might lift you up again
What goes around comes back around, you know
You always reap exactly what you sow.[2]

BELIEF TAKES COURAGE

To step out in faith the way Tim did—to offer to undergo surgery and give a body part to a stranger—took courage.

At that moment, Tim was choosing to fall into the arms of his Father in heaven. He was *believing* that God would catch him and not let him down.

---

2 "Sow Mercy" by Reba Rambo-McGuire and Dony McGuire © 2012 Songs of Rambo McGuire/SESAC. Used by permission. All rights reserved.

And look how the hand of God moved Tim and Don in the directions He wanted them to go:

- He used the song "Sow Mercy" to prompt Don to get out of the car, to spark a conversation, and to establish a bond with Tim.
- Then God used Belinda's plea on Facebook to stir Tim's heart, prompting him to talk with Sherry about what God seemed to be saying to him, that they needed to reach out to Don and Belinda right away.
- Finally, Tim's leap of faith to save Don's life—the strong belief that he was acting in accordance with a nudging from God—also saved his own.

It's not uncommon to feel shy or uncomfortable when we are taking a step of faith to help someone else. But when God prompts you to move out of your comfort zone, He often uses Godwinks to signal that the nudge is from Him.

And when you *believe* that God is at the heart of your actions, even more Godwinks will occur.

> *Whoever sows to please the Spirit,*
> *from the Spirit will reap eternal life.*
> —GALATIANS 6:8 NIV

The principle that your faith in God is essential to having prayers answered and to receiving more Godwinks is further illustrated by Tricia's story, another example of God bringing together two strangers for His purposes.

Tricia and Trish: A Godwink Gift of Love

Tricia's heart flipped. She had been waiting for weeks and weeks. "This is it!" she exclaimed.

The adoption agency had finally called, and the woman said that a darling eighteen-month-old boy was available.

A boy, Tricia thought excitedly. *That's just what I wanted! Another boy!*

Tricia and Dan had always dreamed of having a large family, fondly imagining summer picnics and festive holiday gatherings. They had been well on their way with three girls and a boy when their plans were dashed. Tricia's last delivery was difficult, requiring a C-section and a tubal ligation that closed the door to her having more children biologically.

But Tricia had—in her words—an "unsettled feeling" ever since she had had her last baby. So Tricia and Dan applied to an adoption agency, were approved, and then waited for over two months.

Then came a call from the agency, a call that gave them hope! The plan was foster care at first with an option to adopt, and they promptly sent in the paperwork.

Once again they waited. Time crawled on, weeks and then more weeks, and they didn't hear a word from the agency. Tricia was disappointed, and then she got angry.

"I don't understand You, God! Where in the world is my baby? You know our passionate desire—and You know the needs of this little boy." [3]

As soon as she voiced that prayer, Tricia felt the presence of God.

"My rapid breathing slowed, the anger died . . . I heard His distinct whisper, saying . . . *Trust in Me. Wait upon My time-table. Your son will soon be home.*" [4]

Tricia Seaman is a nurse, and she poured her compassion for others into her work—especially when she was waiting for her boy.

One morning at the hospital Tricia was assigned to a woman

3 Tricia Seaman and Diane Nichols, *God Gave Me You* (Nashville, TN: Howard Publishing, 2016), 25–26.

4 Ibid., 26.

who was just emerging from surgical sedation. Looking at her, Tricia felt an instant empathy. She was strapped down with IVs inserted into the bends of both arms, her hair was disheveled, and she was groggy.

Tricia smiled as she watched the young woman blink her eyes.

"Well, hello there," said Tricia gently. "How are you doing?"

As the patient attempted to respond, "OK" came out like a release of breath.

Tricia had glanced at the chart and noted that her patient had the same first name as hers.

"My name is going to be easy for you to remember. It's Tricia, the same as yours. We even have the same initials: T. S. How about that?"

"Oh, that's neat," the patient said slowly.

"What do you like to be called?"

"Trish. That's what most people call me." Her words were getting clearer now.

"Then that's how we'll keep from confusing ourselves: I'll be Tricia, and you'll be Trish."

"I like that." There was even a slight smile.

Tricia and Trish had bonded immediately.

As a nurse, Tricia was skilled at gently asking questions that provided helpful information, and her engaging personality naturally encouraged people to open up to her. Tricia began with her usual inquiry.

"Tell me about your journey, Trish."

Trish was soon explaining that she had been checked into the hospital for a liver biopsy. She'd been diagnosed with a rare form of cancer. The doctors had thought it was under control, but she'd been having stomach pain. The doctors weren't sure just how complicated Trish's situation was.

Tricia spotted a child's crayon drawings on the side table. One was a red heart with the word *MOM* written in the middle.

"You have a child?"

"My son, Wesley. He's eight." She beamed at the very mention of his name.

"Who's caring for him?"

"Friends . . . and he has a dog," Trish volunteered. "Her name is Molly. She's a big Bernese Mountain Dog. Another friend dog-sits for me. Robbin Babb. Maybe you know her. She's a physical therapist at this hospital."

"Yes, I've met Robbin," said Tricia.

As Trish became fully awake, she clearly needed to talk. She began to confide in Tricia, sharing her worries and fears with greater and greater urgency as she went on.

"I'm a single mom. Wesley's father is out of the picture. He has no grandparents and no close relatives. And if anything ever happened to me . . ."

Her sentence hung in the air without an ending.

Then Trish asked Tricia about *her* family. Since hospital guidelines recommend that healthcare practitioners keep their conversations focused on the patient, Tricia simply said that she was married to Dan and that they had four kids.

Over the next nine or ten days, Tricia was never again assigned to be Trish's attending nurse. But Tricia took every opportunity to pop into her room and see how she was doing. Sometimes she would pray with Trish.

On the day Trish was to be discharged, Tricia went to Trish's room to give her a hug and say good-bye. She found Trish sitting in a chair talking with a social worker, and Tricia could tell by the look on Trish's face that she was not hearing good news.

"Oh, I'll come back," said Tricia quickly.

"No, I'm glad you came by," Trish said, standing up and walking toward her. "The tests came back."

"What did they say?"

"The cancer has spread," said Trish stoically. "I only have a short time to live."

"Oh, Trish," said Tricia, reaching to hug her.

A heavy sadness fell upon Tricia as a powerful sense of empathy rose from within, the kind of empathy only a mother can feel.

Trish was looking straight at Tricia, with a firm voice and no tears, as the most direct and staggering words came from her lips: "I have a question for you. When I die, will you and your husband raise my son?"

The request took Tricia's breath away! She honestly didn't know how to respond. A torrent of thoughts flooded her mind: *You hardly know me . . . What about the father? . . . What are the legal ramifications? . . .*

"Oh, Trish! This is happening so fast . . . You should pray about that . . . Talk to your attorney . . . Don't decide anything right now."

Still reeling from the request of this dying mother, she thought again of a red heart, with the letters *MOM*, drawn by a little boy who would soon have no one.

Tricia hugged Trish again.

"You and Wesley will continue to be in my prayers, Trish." Tricia swallowed hard as she quickly left the room before succumbing to tears.

On her drive home Tricia felt bad for acting so clumsily. Then she realized that she and Trish had never exchanged contact information. There was no way to reach her, and it was against hospital rules to get that kind of information from medical records.

When she arrived home, Tricia sat down with Dan to discuss the sensitive request that this desperate mother had presented. They talked for a while and weren't sure what to do. So they prayed. In the end Dan said, "We need to take this one step at a time. Why don't we see what she needs—groceries, medication. Let's see what we can do to help her."

"Of course. That's a good next step, and we'll go from there." 5

"Where . . . where *could* it go?" said Dan.

Tricia fidgeted with her hands but said nothing.

Dan responded to his own question: "I think we need to trust God with this one and see what's meant to be."

"Are you talking about adoption?" Tricia asked gingerly.

He nodded. "This could be God's way of providing the right little boy we've been waiting for."

They prayed again.

The first task was to figure out how to contact Trish without having any contact information. Then Tricia remembered Molly, the Bernese dog. And Robbin Babb, Tricia's coworker and the dog-sitter used by Trish. Tricia tracked down Robbin at the hospital and explained everything leading up to the question Trish had asked, "When I die, will you and your husband raise my son?"

---

5 Ibid., 14.

Robbin was floored—but she was immediately on board, ready to help, recommending that they go visit Trish together. Having the phone number from Robbin, Tricia called to let Trish know they were coming and to ask what she needed.

Trish was pleased to hear from her.

"Popsicles, please. That's about all I can eat."

After stopping off to buy a few things at Walmart, Tricia and Robbin arrived at a rundown apartment complex.

"Hi," said Trish, opening the door. "Wesley, we have visitors. There's someone I want you to meet."

The eight-year-old came bouncing over to his mother.

"You know Robbin, but this is Tricia. She took care of Mommy when I was in the hospital."

"Hello, Wesley!" said Tricia, as she held out a small basket with candy in it. "I've heard about you. I have a son close to your age. He likes these kinds of jelly beans."

"Wow! Thanks!" said Wesley, helping himself right away.

For the next five or six weeks, Tricia checked in on Trish regularly. Then one day she learned that Trish had been taken to the hospital. When an American Cancer Society volunteer arrived to transport Trish for treatment, Wesley explained that his mother had been sleeping for a long time. The volunteer found Trish on the sofa incoherent. A neighbor agreed to take care of Wesley as the ambulance arrived to rush Trish to the hospital.

Later, when Tricia visited her room, her new friend's eyes were closed. Tricia touched her forehead, and her eyes fluttered open.

"Do you know who I am?" Tricia asked.

There was a long pause.

"Tricia," Trish finally answered. Then she lifted up her head and grabbed Tricia's arm. "Am I dying . . . right now?"

"No. I think you're just very dehydrated from your chemo treatments."

"We still have so much to do," said Trish, laying her head back on the pillow.

Not long after that hospital stay, Mother's Day was approaching. Dan and Tricia decided to invite Trish and Wesley to come to their home, spend the night, and celebrate the holiday with their four children.

All four Seaman kids embraced Wesley right away. Especially Noah, Tricia's only boy, who was just two years younger than Wesley.

Before the Mother's Day visit was over, Trish found an appropriate moment to again ask Tricia and Dan the big question: "Will you two raise my son?"

This time Tricia and Dan were prepared for Trish's bold question. They had spent weeks in conversation with God and each other, trusting that God would give them clarity and a peace in their decision—they *believed* that God was directing their steps.

They both instantly responded, "Yes."

Dan didn't let the conversation end there. He recommended that Trish and Wesley move in with them: Trish would benefit from the assistance, and Wesley would begin to assimilate with his new family.

The next five months were—in the words of Trish—"the best months of my life."

She grew confident that her child would have a secure future and be raised by a wonderful family. She felt loved by Tricia, Dan, and their children as well as by the church and the neighbors who had rallied around the two families and embraced them.

In watching her friend die, Tricia began to appreciate even more the value and blessings of life. She saw how Trish would sit quietly, savoring every moment, smiling as rays of sunshine enveloped her like a cozy blanket, or relishing the playful giggles of her little boy. She watched a mother appreciating the simple joys of life as if the next breath would be her last.

It was a sad day when Trish Somers left our world, but Tricia and Dan were also rejoicing: they knew that Trish was now free of pain as she peacefully and joyfully strolls through God's glorious heaven with peace of mind about her child, who is still on earth.

Now ten years old, Wesley has blended nicely into the Seaman family. Also, Tricia has written the charming book *God Gave Me You*[6] both to honor Trish and to express her gratitude for God's grace and His Godwinks.

Tricia's Godwink was an amazing answer to prayer. She never doubted that God would answer. She *believed* that He had placed the desires in her heart for another son. And that He, in His mysterious ways, would bring her that son. After all, that's what the voice had told her when she was awaiting an eighteen-month-old foster child who never came. That voice had said, *Trust in Me. Wait on My timetable. Your son will soon be home.*

Tricia was fond of asking patients like Trish, "What's your journey?" Now, as Tricia looks back over her own journey, these words from her delightful book sum it up:

What were the chances I'd learn so many lessons from a brief encounter in a hospital room? Who would have guessed a stranger would enter my life and I would be for-ever changed as a mother, a nurse, a wife, and a person?[7]

All of us have had experiences like Tricia's, those times when

---

6 http://www.amazon.com/God-Gave-Me-You-Heaven-Sent/dp/1501131834?ie=UTF8&keywords=tricia%20seaman&qid=1464522624&ref_=sr_1_1&s=books&sr=1-1.

7 Ibid., xiii.

we prayed, but it didn't look like God was going to answer our prayers in the way, or on the timetable, that we wanted. The truth is, God hears our prayers immediately. However, He moves in the spiritual realm so it may take time for the results to manifest in the physical.

God definitely has His reasons for waiting to reveal the answer. Sometimes, for instance, He wants us to continue to seek Him and pray with persistence so our faith will be released.

Whatever you ask for in prayer,
believe *that you have received it,*
and it will be yours.
—MARK 11:24 NIV

Sometimes God is divinely aligning people and circumstances according to His perfect plan. Even though Tricia hoped and prayed that the adoption agency had a child for her, God had a better plan. He not only wanted to bless Tricia with a child, but He also wanted to bless Trish with a family for Wesley.

When you *believe* that God is who He says He is, and that He can do what He says He can do, you are applying Secret #3 for more Godwinks and answered prayer.

SECRET #4

EXPECT

The more you expect *to receive Godwinks and answered prayers, the more you'll be able to see them.*

YOUR EXPECTANCY IS HEALTHY

Normally we use the word *expectant* when we are talking about a woman who is pregnant. But let's use that idea as a metaphor for the larger point we wish to make here.

An expectant mother is excited about the upcoming event that will have a monumental impact on her life. She's counting down the days and is often the center of attention and being showered with gifts.

Mom is not in this alone; there's a father who is often actively involved in labor and delivery, but clearly, Mom is the one who is doing the hard work.

Aside from morning sickness, *expectancy* is a time of joy; mothers can't wait to love and nurture a precious little baby.

As well, expectancy is a good place to be when you're *expecting* something other than a baby.

The coach of a football team, for instance, should exude *expectations* of winning.

In business we are impressed by leaders who not only have clear goals but who project a confident *expectation* of success.

In the context of this book, *expectancy* relates to the biblical promise we mentioned earlier—that whatever you ask in prayer, in accordance with God's will for your life, believing, you can *expect* to receive.

Here are three stories that show what we mean.

~~~

David Oyelowo: Expecting the Godwink

"You will play the role of Martin Luther King."

The imaginary *Hollywood Reporter* headline running through David's mind was too preposterous even to think about, let alone to say aloud to anyone else: "Little-known British Actor David Oyelowo (*o-yellow-o*) Tapped to Play Martin Luther King."

Anyone he told would think he'd gone mad.

Yet, as David read the script about his hero—eight years before the MLK movie *Selma* opened—he was overcome with a powerful sense that he had heard the voice of God in his spirit.

He prayed about it. *Is that You, God?*

David was shocked—he couldn't believe it—so he wrote it down. "On July 24th, 2007, God told me I was going to play Dr. King in this film."

At that moment David began the journey God wants for each of us. After all, He says we must ask in prayer; believe with an unwavering faith; and then, having done everything we can possibly do, simply entrust the situation to Him—to His timing, His actions, His divine organizing—and *expect* to receive the answer to your prayer.

David Oyelowo was not new in his relationship with God. He was sixteen when he accepted Christ as his Savior. "I do know God's voice," David says with a smile. Reflecting on the moment he heard God's promise, "my spirit didn't doubt it" even if human reason was more skeptical.

David auditioned for the part.

He didn't get it.

Five of the seven directors who were in charge of the film for the next several years maintained that David was not right for the role.

"My soul was like, OK, I understand," he recalls. In his heart, though, he knew he'd already been *given* the part; he just needed to keep *expecting* it.

David kept getting passed over, yet he kept on *expecting*.

When you see absolutely no evidence that your prayers are being answered, it's difficult to keep your faith strong. But later, when we look back, we can always see that God was getting people and events into proper alignment. That was surely the case with the film *Selma*, and God also needed to prepare David for the role of Dr. King.

That preparation came in David's roles in other films. In *Lincoln* he played a union soldier who asked the Civil War president for the right to vote. David was a fighter pilot in *Red Tails* and a preacher in *The Help*. David's role in *The Butler* gave him—an Englishman—insight into what it meant to be an African-American.

Then one day God's prophetic word was finally fulfilled. When director Lee Daniels joined the film project, he offered David the role!

Thank You, God!

David's prayer was answered; his faith rewarded; his *expectation* realized.

Under the direction of Ava DuVernay, *Selma* received wonderful reviews and David Oyelowo earned a Golden Globe Best Actor nomination.

During the filming, David and the crew felt God's presence and experienced Godwinks almost daily.

For instance, the day David was to shoot a major Martin Luther King Jr. speech, the set designer was troubled. A lectern had been placed on the set, but he had a spiritual nudge that it ought to be a pulpit.

Recalling there was a church just down the street, he walked the short distance, entered Dexter Avenue Baptist Church, and asked if he could borrow a pulpit.

The person he spoke to said, "Well, you can't have the one in the church, but two days ago we found an old pulpit in the basement. You can use that one."

Shortly thereafter the Godwink was revealed: *that* was the actual pulpit Dr. Martin Luther King had spoken from fifty years earlier when he was delivering the very same speech that David Oyelowo was giving on that day!

"Wow!" says David. "The same pulpit, and it was uncovered in the basement only two days before!"

With a smile he added, "It was like God was winking at us."
David Oyelowo had asked, believed, and *expected*.

If you don't ask in faith,
don't expect the Lord
to give you any solid answer.
—JAMES 1:5—6

Paul Osteen: Surprises of Expectancy

Have I gotten in over my head, God?

That was a prevailing question on the mind of Dr. Paul Osteen as he and his wife, Jennifer, drove through North Carolina traffic toward Charlotte Airport for their flight back to Houston.

They were leaving a well-attended, smartly produced event at the Cove, the Asheville Conference Center of the Billy Graham Evangelistic Association. Osteen couldn't help but compare that impressive, well-organized, and well-executed conference with the one that he himself was heading up in Houston in just ninety days.

Called Mobilizing Medical Missions—M3 for short—

Paul's event was designed to challenge and encourage health-care professionals to serve the needs of underserved, vulnerable people in developing nations.

The conference had seemed like such a good idea. But with less than three months to go, he had thirty-five speakers booked and only thirty-four people signed up to attend!

God, am I doing the right thing? Will my conference be a colossal failure? Will I embarrass myself and my family?

Osteen couldn't shake those thoughts.

Self-doubt was uncharacteristic for Dr. Paul Osteen. In the operating room, where he had successfully performed general and vascular surgery for many years, he was always cool and confident.

Yet as he drove, his mind drifted to a time shortly before his dad died. Paul had confided to his medical colleagues in Little Rock that he loved his life—his God, his wife and family, and his work as a surgeon—yet he was somehow feeling disenchanted. Paul's associates suggested that he was burned out. But was he?

When Paul heard the news of his father's sudden death, a strong inner voice spoke to him, nudging him to do something highly illogical: leave his thriving medical practice, move back to Houston, and help his family pick up the reins of the ministry his father and mother had built at Lakewood Church.

Really, God?

To the dismay of his friends and colleagues, Paul obeyed the voice and left Arkansas.

Paul's brother Joel stepped into the Lakewood Church pulpit, and Paul took on the task of overseeing all the ministries. The Osteen family pulled together, doing what they felt they had to do. But they had no idea what was about to happen. They would not have imagined that the church would erupt, growing from a sizable five thousand members to being hailed as the largest church in America. Regular weekly attendance increased ten times and more, and their international television ministry reached into hundreds of millions of homes around the globe.

After several years—once Paul was confident that the ministry staff had matured enough to allow him some time away—he and Jennifer were drawn to the idea of participating in extended medical missions and taking their kids with them for several months a year to places where medical care was greatly needed.

"My passion for surgery came back with a vengeance," recalls Paul.

These God-inspired trips allowed him to perform surgery in remote areas of Africa. There, one doctor remarked that Paul was the only surgeon in an area the size of Louisiana.

Upon returning home from that trip, Paul came across a report that in one single zip code in Houston there were twenty-five hundred physicians. He contrasted that with the comment the doctor in Africa had made.

The seed of an idea was sown. *What if we could encourage each of those twenty-five hundred physicians, nurses, and other health professionals to give a little time every year to medical missions?*

What was needed, it seemed to Paul, was a "clearinghouse of information," a conference where other medical people—who, like Paul, had been to those developing nations—could share their passion to help others.

Now fast-forward.

Paul was on the threshold of birthing the first of those conferences. He sensed it could be big, very big . . . but he also had a nagging thought: a big flop.

M3—Mobilizing Medical Missions—was soon on the calendar. It would be held at Lakewood Church. The first thirty-five of forty speakers were locked in, and word had gone out to hundreds of potential exhibitors.

But only thirty-four attendees had signed up?

Paul was worried. And his concerns grew every day as the conference day drew closer.

As Paul and Jennifer drove their rental car through North

Carolina traffic, the two of them decided that they needed to pray specifically about attendance. Ever since he was a kid, Paul had known the undeniable power of prayer. His father had told him about Christ's promise, that whatever we ask for in prayer—believing—we can *expect* to receive. He also knew that it was sometimes God's will to give us something better than what we had in mind.

But was Paul really *expecting* to receive the number of attendees he had been planning for?

Paul thought about the encouragement he had received from his staff—headed by Lori Bethran, who had considerable experience in running conferences—and reminded himself that they knew what they were talking about. They had counseled him to have patience, to have faith.

Still, that was hard when you were looking at thirty-four tickets sold.

As they prayed, both Paul and Jennifer felt an inner stirring to shift their attention from the circumstances—the handful of people who had responded—to the work for God that the M3 conference would be initiating.

In that instant, Paul and Jennifer saw the extraordinary Godwink. The license plate on the car that pulled right in front of them communicated a message as clearly as a person-to-person call, directly from God:

The plate read FOCUS M3.

Paul and Jennifer blinked. Wide-eyed, they looked at each other and smiled.

"That Godwink encouraged me to keep going, to get down to the steel in my soul. Don't give up!" said Paul. He knew that the source of their encouragement was none other than God Himself!

Acknowledge him, and He shall direct your paths.
—PROVERBS 3:6 KJV

Paul realized that, although he was one out of seven billion people on the planet, God chose to connect directly with him at that moment. To lift him up. Reassure him that, because he was going forward with faith and doing God's work, all would be well.

When Paul and Jennifer saw the FOCUS M3 license plate, everything for the M3 conference started to turn around. Day by day the situation started looking better. Paul began to think, *God's going to surprise me*.

Paul and Jennifer had asked for God's assistance, they believed that He could do what He promised, and they now *expected* a positive outcome.

Within thirty days, hundreds of people were signing up

every week. When the M3 conference finally took place, over 1,850 medical people were in attendance! Exhibitors were euphoric, one saying that the number of referrals they got in one day would normally take several months.

The first Mobilizing Medical Missions conference was a huge success.

Secret #4 to more Godwinks and answered prayers is this:

Maintain Your Expectancy *That God Is Going to Come Through for You!*

A POSTSCRIPT WITH AN EXCLAMATION POINT!

The day I called to interview Paul for this story, God winked in another delightfully amazing way.

As Paul's assistant put me on hold to bring him to the phone, I listened to the live feed of Joel Osteen's radio program. At that very moment Joel was saying, "We shouldn't lose our *expectancy*. Whatever God started in your life, He is going to finish."

How about that? Can you calculate the odds that Joel would speak those very words about *expectancy* on the radio, the exact second I was waiting to speak to his brother about *expectancy*?

We know, of course, that we can't put odds on what God will do. When we acknowledge Him, He acknowledges us.

Paul and Jennifer acknowledged God as they prayed that morning on the North Carolina highway and a license plate appeared right in front of them, bearing the exact name of their conference—M3—and reaffirming the decision they had just made: to FOCUS.

Take heart from Paul's astonishing Godwinks. If you are heading toward what you believe is God's destiny for you, He will surely place signs along the highway of life to keep you on the path. He will provide Godwinks of reassurance.

In a different take on *expectancy*, we close this chapter with a sweet story from Kevin.

Kevin Fortney: Six Words Dad Wanted to Hear

"I first heard Dad say those six words when I was thirteen," says Kevin Fortney.

"I looked at him as my tower of strength. He had deep blue eyes, he stood tall, and he spoke in a commanding yet gentle voice. He said, 'When I die and stand before my heavenly Father, there are only six words I need to hear.'"

That *expectant* statement was a seed planted in a corner of Kevin's mind, and it took root there.

Through the years Kevin never stopped learning from his dad, a highly successful oil and gas attorney who truly lived every day as a Christian gentleman.

"He was an imposing man with a dignified and confident air about him," says Kevin. "I wanted to emulate him in every way I could. He was my idol, my mentor, my counselor, my best friend. Anyone could see the love and the strength of God in him."

When cancer attacked his father at the age of fifty-six, Kevin was thirty-two. It was a shock to learn that a fast-moving lung cancer had invaded his father's body. And he was a man who had never smoked.

"Still, Dad hung on to his faith. Because he did, so did I."

Only a few months later, Kevin's dad died. Utterly crushed, Kevin cried out to God in desperate prayer. He lay on his bed weeping in inconsolable agony. He didn't understand why God had let his dad die, and at such an early age. Kevin couldn't make sense of it.

The depth of his pain was unfamiliar and unwelcome. For the first time Kevin experienced the raw truth that none of us is prepared for grief. We may be intellectually positioned for death, but emotionally, we are ill-equipped when it arrives.

"God, I need to know two things," Kevin said, his voice cracking and his eyes hurting from weeping and being so tightly closed. "I need to know, God . . . is this really Your will? Had Dad really fulfilled his purpose here? And, God . . ."

He heard an involuntary wail rise from his throat.

"Did he hear those words from You? Those six words he so longed to hear?"

Kevin poured out his tears, overcome by heart-wrenching pain.

When Kevin's sobs quieted, muscles that had been squeezing his eyes closed began to relax. Opening his eyes slightly, he looked around the bedroom. His vision was blurry. A black object came into view. He reached for it, ashamed that he hadn't opened it for many months.

With the Bible in his lap, he pulled himself to a sitting position, slowly opening the book as if it were a treasure chest. A bookmark with writing on it fell out, but his attention was drawn more to the color yellow on the page from which the bookmark fell. Highlighted in yellow were six words: "Well done, good and faithful servant."

Kevin cried again. This time, with wails of satisfaction. God had answered his prayer.

Those were the only six words his dad had longed to hear from his heavenly Father. When Kevin saw those words, he knew that his Dad had indeed received his reward from the God he loved so dearly, and by knowing that, Kevin also received the peace and comfort he needed to carry on.

A day or two later at the memorial service, he told a somber but attentive audience, "Dad used to say that life was about receiving gifts from God, holding on to them, and then letting them go. What a precious gift he was."

Kevin then quoted from the bookmark that dropped from the Bible: "Have no fear. God will either shield you from suffering or give you unfailing strength to bear it."

An Afterthought

Kevin's dad modeled what God desires from each of us: He wants us to *ask* in prayer, *believe* in Him with all our heart, and *expect* to receive His favor.

But when Kevin and his dad—together with his mom and the rest of the family—prayed for complete healing and it didn't happen, Kevin was tormented by human questions: *Why, God? And why now? Dad was young.*

In the end Kevin accepted that he had received a partial answer to those questions. Through a Godwink, the Lord reassured Kevin that his father's death was indeed according to

God's will and timing. Kevin will have to wait until he sees God face-to-face to fully understand why his dad was graduated to heaven so early in his life.

Let us be mindful, though, that at graduations, the graduate is not the one feeling regret or sadness. The graduate, after all, is in the glorious presence of God. At graduations, the ones to feel sadness are those who are left behind.

> *We shall see face to face.*
> *Now I know in part;*
> *then I shall know fully.*
> — I CORINTHIANS 13:12 NIV

IN SUM

Actor David Oyelowo—against all rational human reasoning—*expected* to be given the role of Martin Luther King.

Dr. Paul Osteen, bolstered by the Godwink of seeing the FOCUS M3 license plate, *expected*, against all logical deductions from current ticket sales, that his M3 conference would turn out fine.

Kevin Fortney *expected* that once he was convinced that his Dad had heard the six words his father had said he hoped to hear from God—"Well done, good and faithful servant"—that he, Kevin, would feel a peace about his dad's early death.

In each case these men had *asked* in prayer, *believed* in the omnipotence and omniscience of God, but also *expected* to have their prayers answered. And answered they were—Godwink by Godwink.

SECRET #5

SIGNS

During uncertain and trying times, God winks at you with signs *that provide comfort and reassurance. Developing eyes that see the* signs *will increase your awareness of Godwinks and answered prayer.*

"SEND ME A SIGN!"

How many times in your life have you said, "God, please send me a sign"?

It's a common appeal. We want heavenly confirmation that we are on the right track or making the right decision.

In the ancient Scriptures, the phrase *signs and wonders*

occurs sixteen times in the New Testament alone, and it nearly always refers to the miracles of Christ. Of course He knew that, as humans, we sometimes want reassurance via the supernatural.

There's the biblical account of the royal official who went to Jesus saying that his son was close to death and begging Christ to go with him and heal the boy. Before replying "Go, your son will live," Jesus observed, "Unless you people see *signs* and *wonders* . . . you will never believe" (John 4:48, 50 NIV).

In this chapter, we will see Godwinks that have occurred as signs, and in the next chapter, we'll talk about wonders.

One of our favorite stories about the power of signs was told to us by a much-loved Christian writer.

※

Karen Kingsbury's Sign from Dad

It was a gorgeous autumn day in New York City.

Karen Kingsbury had become America's number one inspirational novelist. Her books had surpassed twenty-five million titles sold. The CEO of Simon & Schuster Publishing had just treated her royally in celebration of that milestone. Now it was time to enjoy the remainder of the day with her daughter, Kelsey, and son-in-law, Kyle.

As they entered the elevator on an upper floor of the Sixth Avenue skyscraper, Karen smiled inwardly and felt that familiar impulse to call her biggest fan. As with every other significant moment in her life, she couldn't wait to hear her dad's joy and picture the happy tears creeping into his eyes.

For the smallest instant, she began to reach for her phone. *Stop!*

How long would she automatically reach for the telephone only to collide with the cold reality and deep sadness that he was gone? A sudden heart attack had taken him away months before.

Lord, please tell Dad that I love him.

Saying a silent prayer was all she could do on a crowded elevator. She had, however, trained herself to make her mind switch from sad to glad, the way she was encouraged to do by a line in her dad's favorite song: "Fill my heart with gladness; take away all my sadness."

She smiled as she thought about that day he called and enthusiastically announced that he had just heard a song on the radio by Rod Stewart that perfectly expressed how he felt about his family.

He began to sing "Have I told you lately that I love you . . ."!

There, in the snapshot in her mind, his voice was brimming with love as he said, "That song is exactly how I feel about you, your mom, and our family." In the years that followed, he often talked about the song, sometimes with tears in his eyes.

Rod Stewart's song took on a life of its own, weaving itself into Karen's heart and every special occasion. In a string of Godwinks the melody popped up here, there, and everywhere—after her son's school play, in the Bahamas during a family vacation, and on the set of the first movie based on one of her books. The song had been such an expression of Karen's and her father's deep affection for each other that she'd had the words "Have I Told You Lately That I Love You" etched on his gravestone.

Karen, Kelsey, and Kyle stepped from the quiet of the Simon & Schuster building into the cacophony of New York's Sixth Avenue. "Hey, we have time! Why don't we go to that park Carolyn mentioned?" said Karen, opening the door of the cab.

Simon & Schuster CEO Carolyn Reidy had suggested they visit one of her favorite NYC sanctuaries, High Line Park. Within just twenty minutes, Karen, Kelsey, and Kyle were strolling the plush and picturesque paths of the greenbelt that had been built on what was once an elevated railroad track overlooking the Hudson River.

"Let's get a picture," said Karen, and she took a couple shots of Kelsey and Kyle. Then she held the camera at arm's length, hoping for a decent three-person selfie. It wasn't working.

"Can I take that for you?" said a man with a mellow voice

who "just happened" to be passing by with a woman on his arm.

"Oh, thank you," said Karen, as Kelsey showed him which button to push. Stylishly attired in a sweater and jeans, the gentleman framed the shot, snapped the picture, and studied it for a moment. "That's lovely!" He smiled as he handed the camera back. "Thank you," said everyone in unison.

As the man and woman strolled away, Kelsey leaned close to Karen and whispered with tempered urgency, "Mom! Do you know who that was?" Karen's eyes widened. "It was Rod Stewart. When I showed him how to use the camera, he said, 'I'm usually on the other side of this thing, but this is fun too!'"

A sense of disbelief rushed over Karen. She turned around and saw that the two of them were still on the pathway. She didn't want to look like a crazy person, but she felt an overwhelming urge to catch up to him. So she ran.

"Sir! Sir!" she said breathlessly, stepping close so as not to be heard by others. "Are you . . . Rod Stewart?"

He smiled and put his hand on her arm.

"Yes."

"I have to tell you about my father," she blurted out.

As she told her story, how her Dad used Rod's song as a commemoration of his love for his family, how that song just seemed to show up at auspicious moments, and that its lyric is engraved on her dad's gravestone, tears formed in Rod Stewart's eyes. He put his hands together as if he were praying, and he lifted them toward heaven. Then his eyes met Karen's again. "You just made my day," he said. "May I give you a hug?"

As they said their good-byes and walked in opposite directions, Karen, Kelsey, and Kyle lingered on a park bench, savoring the moment and the grace of God that they had just experienced. They marveled at how God knows exactly what we need and how He causes us—despite astronomical odds against it—to be in exactly the right place at the right moment for His purposes to be achieved.

Their questions were rapid-fire:

"What if Carolyn Reidy had not suggested we visit High Line Park?"

"What if we had walked just a bit slower and hadn't been there, at that precise moment, to intersect with Rod Stewart?"

"What if Karen hadn't wanted a group selfie?"

Here's another question: Why was Rod Stewart at a park built on an old railroad trestle? Is he infatuated with railroads? It turns out that he is.

At his home in Los Angeles, he has elaborate model layouts replicating New York Central and Pennsylvania Railroads in the 1940s. He has similar models with English trains at his home in Britain.

When you open your eyes to the Godwinks woven by divine alignment into your everyday existence, you discover that God is downright astonishing. And the closer you get to Him, the better you understand the lyrics to the song that God Himself is singing to you: "Have I told you lately that I love you?"

And at the end of the day
We should give thanks and pray
To the One, to the One.

AFTERTHOUGHTS

Rod Stewart didn't "just happen" to be at High Line Park at the perfect moment. There are no random happenings in God's grand plan. God had already intended for him to intersect with Karen's life at that precise moment, to give her a *sign* of hope and encouragement.

God lets us know that we are on a divine GPS—God's Positioning System. He sees every tear and He feels every hurt as He comforts us by weaving Godwinks into our times of sorrow. Each Godwink invites us to trust Him more, and the more frequently we acknowledge His Godwinks, the more often we will see them.

Karen's Godwink turned her sadness into joy. God used Rod Stewart to remind Karen that her dad was at complete peace, at home in heaven with our Creator. One day Karen will see him again—and what a glorious time it will be!

When you feel sad and lonely, hold tightly to the promise that you too will see your loved ones again. In the meantime, ask God to give you *signs* so you don't miss His Godwinks of hope and comfort.

There is a time for everything . . .
a time to weep and a time to laugh,
a time to mourn and a time to dance.
—ECCLESIASTES 3:1, 4 NIV

Vin's Sign from the Past

Vin Di Bona, creator of *America's Funniest Home Videos*, one of TV's longest-running series, was visiting his mom in Rhode Island.

It was a beautiful Sunday afternoon, perfect for a nostalgic drive through old neighborhoods that stirred memories of long ago. They were on their way to the cemetery where Vin's dad was buried.

Vin had a sudden urge. "Hey, let's swing past Bain."

His car crept slowly to the curb as he pulled up in front of the traditional brick school building where he had gone to junior high. He pictured himself walking through the front doors fifty years before.

Wistfully he said, "Just think of all the dreams that were born there, Mom."

His elegant mother, wearing one of her stylish hats and looking like she'd just come from a garden club luncheon, thought for a moment. Then she spoke softly. "Yes. That's where your dream to be in show business was born."

She's right, Vin thought, his mind flashing to Mrs. MacDonald, a teacher who encouraged him with the words "Reach for the stars!"

Vin turned his car away from the curb, glad he'd gone a little out of their way to reconnect with this significant symbol of his past.

The next day, while Vin was waiting to board a plane back to Los Angeles, he had time to check in with his assistant, Melissa.

"You received a sweet letter from a thirteen-year-old boy

who attends your old school in Cranston," she reported, "and a note from his special ed teacher."

"My old school? Bain Junior High?"

"Yes, I guess so," she replied, glancing at the letter to confirm the name.

"I was just there yesterday! For the first time in fifty years!" What were the odds of these two things happening in two days, back-to-back?

"What was the letter about?"

"The boy's name is Cesar. He said he was in the library and checked out a book: *Uncle Remus: His Songs and Sayings*. It was an old book . . . so old it had a library card in the back. When he looked at the card, he saw that the person who checked out the book in April 1959 was Vin Di Bona."

"I did? That's amazing."

Vin was touched. He listened as Melissa read the accompanying note from Tanya Murphy, Cesar's special education teacher. She described Cesar as a "very shy" student with communication challenges who had recently arrived at Bain and didn't have a lot of friends yet. But Cesar loved to read, and he spent most of his free time in the school library.

When Cesar checked out *Uncle Remus*, he asked the librarian, Mrs. Shore, why there was a card in the back with names on it. She explained that before computers, those cards were used to keep track of who borrowed which book. She then noted that one of the book's previous readers, years before, was a now-famous TV producer who grew up in their area, Vin Di Bona.

Tanya Murphy was in the library with Cesar and suggested that he write Vin a letter. She turned it into a project, which led Cesar to an old yearbook, so they made copies of a couple of pictures of Vin to include in the letter. When Cesar doubted that he would get a reply, Tanya became his encourager, saying, "What have you got to lose?"

A few days later Vin wrote to Cesar and Tanya, saying he was touched by their notes and explained that he was certain they had been part of a Godwink. Vin also invited the two of them and Cesar's mom on an all-expense-paid trip to Los Angeles to tour the TV studio and then watch the taping of an episode of *America's Funniest Home Videos*!

For Cesar, his mom, and his teacher, it was a once-in-a-lifetime experience. They were picked up in a limousine, treated like VIPs, given front-row seats during the taping of *AFHV*, and then taken to Disneyland.

When he returned to Bain Junior High a few days later, Cesar found that he was no longer just the shy special needs kid in the library. The kids treated him like a Hollywood celebrity! More important, Cesar had learned an important lesson about stepping out in faith—"What have you got to lose?" He had written a letter, not hoping for much in return, yet look what had resulted.

Vin wrote Tanya Murphy a description of Godwinks: "They are events in our lives that are not just happenstance but are destined by God. Wow! One happened to Cesar and me."

AFTERTHOUGHT

No matter how successful Vin Di Bona had become in Hollywood television production, this was a singular moment of astonishment. It was profoundly personal because it occurred in the company of his dear mother as they were en route to pay homage to Vin's father. It was baffling why he received an inner nudge to drive by his old junior high school in Cranston, for the first time in fifty years, on the very eve of a letter arriving at his LA office from a boy attending that same school and who had selected the same book Vin had read decades before. The odds of these circumstances were incalculable! But what did all this mean?

Vin is certain the experience was a Godwink *sign*.

We are not privy to all that was going on in Vin's life at that moment or what Cesar may have been wrestling with, but we can conclude that the Godwink *sign* was a boost of encouragement to both.

GETTING A NUDGE

Did you notice that in both Karen's story and Vin's, they each felt a nudge to do something? Does that happen to you at times? When it does, do you act on the nudge, or do you dismiss it?

God will often nudge us nonverbally in order to lead us to do something He wants us to do something or to be where He wants us to be. God gently nudged Karen and Vin and brought positive results, but in some cases God warns us of a dangerous situation with an urgent nudge.

There are countless stories of people who averted car accidents because of a sudden nudge to pull over to the side of the road. When we acknowledge God's presence in our lives and talk with Him daily, we will be able to hear and feel those little tugs. Don't ignore them. God is talking to you.

POSTSCRIPT

A couple of months after Cesar's trip to LA, Vin scheduled a last-minute visit to Boston and decided to swing down to Rhode Island to see his mom again. He asked Melissa to contact the principal at Bain Junior High School, Jenny Chan-Remka, to see if it would be OK for him to stop by that following Monday to say hello.

To his surprise, when he arrived at the school, Vin was greeted with a huge banner with his name on it. It hung across the auditorium stage, the school band was playing "Celebrate," students and teachers were cheering, and the mayor of Cranston read a proclamation of honor!

Here we can see that Godwink *signs* have an aftereffect: each wink can prompt countless ripples that touch the lives of many other people.

SIGNS ARE NOT DECISION MAKERS

Godwink *signs* encourage you and affirm that God is right there with you. They can be especially encouraging if you are facing tough decisions and going through hard times.

But it must be said that Godwinks—in and of themselves—

should never be used as a crutch for the decisions you need to make while in consultation with God. Godwinks are not God's way of telling you to take this job or marry that guy. Instead, Godwinks are simply encouragers, reminding you that God is at your side. When you remember that God is always there, your decisions are more likely to result in a proper course of action.

That was surely the case in this next story when Louise and I faced a major decision. Louise recounts the story:

Godwinks and the Dream House

SQuire and I are blessed to live in one of the most beautiful places on earth—Martha's Vineyard. I have a special fondness for the island in part because my family settled here four generations ago. They were fishermen and farmers who became part of the fabric of this iconic spot.

As a child, I felt such joy spending every summer with my loving grandparents. I have a treasure trove of memories that I'll cherish forever.

In my twenties, I moved from New England to Los Angeles to work in the entertainment field. More than a decade passed before I was able to revisit my island of childhood joy. I often thought about the pristine blue water and the crisp fresh air. I missed the scent of beach roses and the sight of hydrangeas peeking through white picket fences. But I knew in my heart that, one day, I would move back and spend the rest of my life there.

Little did I know that God was going to surprise me with the best Godwink ever—a man by the name of SQuire Rushnell, who I sensed was my mate for life. But deep in my heart, I wondered: *How would he feel about Martha's Vineyard?*

SQuire was the network executive at ABC in charge of Saturday morning television programs, for which he was developing a program called *The Krofft Supershow*. He had suggested to the producers that they hire me after he saw my performance as Witcheepoo in a production of *H. R. Pufnstuf* at Madison Square Garden. That was my first step in a long career in show business.

From my home in Los Angeles I occasionally had a reason to contact SQuire, calling his ABC office in New York.

Time passed, and I eventually moved from LA to NYC to do a Broadway show called *Dreamstuff*.

One day SQuire surprised me when he was attending a performance of the show. We hadn't seen each other in many years. We went out for coffee and discovered we were both unmarried. We began a courtship. But before getting too serious, I wanted SQuire to see the place of my fondest childhood memories, Martha's Vineyard. I prayed that he would fall in love with the island and that, one day, we would live there happily ever after.

My prayer was answered! SQuire not only loved the island, but he proposed to me at the very location where we hoped to build our dream house. The building site we had chosen was a wonderful piece of property that overlooked the harbor and ocean.

We got ourselves an architect and a builder, and we began the process. We agreed on a price for the completion of construction and took out the maximum loan allowed by the bank. It was a big stretch for us financially, but we felt that if we tightened our belts, we could do it. That is, until the builder doubled the price!

Only the frame of the house was standing when our builder called to say, "I'm sorry, but I have some bad news. The price of building material has skyrocketed, and construction is going to cost you a lot more. A whole lot more—almost twice as much."

We were shocked.

"We are at the very limit of our ability to get funding," we explained. "We maxed out with the bank. What can we do?"

He looked at us and said, "Well, you can sell the house as is, but I need to know. If you're not going to move forward, I have to pull my guys off the job."

We liked our builder, but we also understood that business was business. We were in a bind and didn't know what to do about it.

In our hearts we knew there was no earthly way we could get the money we needed to finish building our home. Funding would have to come from a divine Source—and He had always looked out for us. The money would have to come directly from God.

That's when we buckled down in our prayers. We beseeched God for help. We brought our empty savings account before Him, laid hands on the bank book, and prayed that He would multiply the dollars like He multiplied the loaves and fishes to feed the multitudes (Matthew 14:17–21). Jesus had performed that miracle two thousand years earlier to show people His power and ability to meet their needs. Now, SQuire and I needed His power and help.

We acknowledged before God that the house we were building was His property anyway, and that we were unable to depend on our own resources to keep the project going. But, we told Him as we prayed, we knew we *could* depend on His resources. So we released our grip on our dream home and, in a bigger way than we had before, transferred total ownership to Him.

It was at that point that we felt the Holy Spirit speaking to us. He was saying that if we would use this house to serve Him and serve others, God would do what His Word says He will do: "God will meet all your needs according to the riches of his glory in Christ Jesus" (Philippians 4:19 NIV).

We had absolutely no concrete evidence that God was going to supply our needs, but we had faith that He would. SQuire and I were living out what the Scripture says: "Faith is the substance of things hoped for, the evidence of things not seen" (Hebrews 11:1 KJV).

We brought our request before God and said, "Lord, we are confident that You are going to complete this house, but we would like a definitive *sign* of confirmation that continuing the building project is Your will."

The next day we went to the mailbox hoping against hope that we'd have an unexpected check that would help with the costs—or at least something that would encourage us. But the only things in the box were bills and a letter from the surveyor with a drawing of the plot plan for our house.

As we stared at the drawing, our eyes welled up with tears.

You see, we had pictured our dream home in our minds from every angle, or so we thought.

We knew where every window would go and where every electrical plug would be placed. We had studied the blueprint from the north, east, west, and south, but we had never seen the house from above, from God's perspective. Well, when looked at from above, our dream home was in the shape of a cross!

We knew that the surveyor's drawing was a Godwink! It was the *sign* we'd asked God for, the *sign* confirming that we *should* move forward. We didn't dare tell the builder that we didn't yet know how we were going to pay for it, but we did ask him to get going and to plan on finishing the job.

We knew the only way the cost of construction would be covered was if God did something supernatural.

We had prayed about it and we kept praying. We also believed God was listening to us, and we expected Him to provide. And now we'd gotten our *sign*—that surveyor's drawing of the cross.

Still, I'll admit, fear continued to creep in.

We knew that failure to make our payments would mean that the bank could come in at any moment and take the house. So instead of thinking about that very real possibility, we chose to hang on to *God's* reality. We chose faith in Him. Every time doubt entered our minds, we chased it away with more prayer. The more we prayed, the better we felt. And the more we leaned on God, the more we sensed a supernatural peace.

Two days later the phone rang. The area code was unfamiliar to me.

It was Steve Rosen, a man who had once hired me to do a show in Atlantic City. He was now living in Biloxi, Mississippi. I hadn't heard from him in several years.

Steve said, "Listen, Louise, I'm closing a show at one of my theaters in Gulfport. I need something in there right away, and your name just popped into my mind. Do you think you can get a show up and running in four weeks?"

Before he finished his sentence, I shouted, "*Yes!*"

Then the second Godwink happened. I quickly calculated in my mind and realized that the amount of money he was offering for a one-year contract was exactly what we needed to complete work on the house!

For the next year I lived in Gulfport, Mississippi, performing ten shows a week, while construction of our dream home on the Vineyard was completed.

The day SQuire and I moved in, we prayed over every corner of the house and thanked God for His awesome favor!

Here are some of the lessons we learned by trusting God to provide a *sign* via a Godwink:

- Keep praying even when you don't see results right away.

- Trust that God will release His power to align with your prayers.
- Prayer moves requests from heaven to earth.
- God allows difficulty to grow your faith so you will trust Him more.

SQuire and I often look back on our faith journey and see clearly how God graciously sent Godwinks at the very moments we needed them most.

If you are going through uncertain times, be patient. God knows what He's doing in your life. You can't see the end result, but He can. Your difficulties and delays will one day be cleared away. Keep trusting in the Lord and resist giving up.

Our motto: Pray, pray, and then pray some more. When you do, you'll better understand how powerful God really is and how Godwinks are most often birthed from prayer.

Every house is built by someone,
but God is the builder of everything.

—HEBREWS 3:4 NIV

~~~~~~

Lisa's Sign of the Scarf

Only in her late twenties, Lisa was already creating her unique brand as an artist—L. A. Brown, Photographer, Martha's Vineyard. She had dabbled with oil painting, ceramics, and silk screening, all of which helped her develop a sensitivity to color, shape, and design, and now her photos were hanging in art galleries.

Lisa's dad—Philip James Brown Jr.—was her biggest cheerleader. She always smiled about his high school graduation gift to her. He had bought her a brick of film and a ticket to Martha's Vineyard.

"Just go! Go and shoot pictures. That's what's in your heart!" he said.

It would be hard to find a word to describe her dad. *Robust*, perhaps. He was a robust encourager for every member of the family—his wife, his four daughters, and his two sons.

"Enjoy it while it lasts," he was fond of saying. And "You can't take it with you!"

When the kids had all left the nest and his business was flourishing, Philip and Eileen, Lisa's mom, moved to London and lived there for nearly a decade. He frequently flew the children over to visit, or he sent them on their own adventures to exotic places.

Philip was particularly fond of purchasing thoughtful gifts for members of the family. For instance, to mark special occasions, he gave an exquisite Hermès scarf to each of the women in his family—his mother, his sister (Lisa's "Aunt Nan"), and each of Lisa's sisters. Ranging in cost from three hundred to nine hundred dollars, every scarf was a work of art with a colorful theme—equestrian, tennis, butterflies—that befit the wearer. The scarfs were classy, elegant, and very beautiful, but not quite a fit with Lisa's artsy style.

As she was approaching her thirtieth birthday, she and her dad were shopping on London's posh Sloane Street.

"I want to get you a Hermès scarf for your birthday," he said joyfully. "Let's pick one out."

Uh-oh. The amorphous thought that sooner or later this day would arrive had long lurked in the back of Lisa's mind, and even less clear was any idea of how she would handle it. She found out: she handled it clumsily.

"Oh, Dad . . . I . . . I really appreciate it . . . but, you know, I'm an artist. This is not my thing . . . I don't want you spending that kind of money. You know . . . it's just not my look."

She immediately began to feel remorse. *Did I just hurt Dad's feelings?*

If she did, her dad masked it, and instead for her birthday he gave her a hand-painted scarf with playful colorful circus scenes, which was definitely not as formal or as pricey as a Hermès scarf.

And Lisa loved that scarf. Whenever she wore it, she appreciated that her dad had taken the time to find just the right scarf for her. She treasured that gift from her dad.

Only two years later Lisa's dad died of leukemia.

She was devastated.

"I had two choices," she reflected later. "I could shrivel up and remain in a fetal position. Or I could take stock of my life and honor my father's vision of me. I was very close to both choices."

Lisa prayed. She asked her heavenly Father how she should honor her earthly father.

After that prayer Lisa felt a deep conviction that she must honor her father by being the best photographer she could be. As she pursued her passion, she would fulfill the hopes and dreams he had held for her to be an accomplished photographic artist.

Twenty years later, Lisa Brown Langley and her husband, Brendan, were visiting her mother in New Jersey. They went to the upscale Short Hills Mall to contemplate gift choices for Lisa's impending fiftieth birthday. They browsed past Gucci purses, Prada shoes, and Louis Vuitton bags.

They came upon a Hermès shop. "Let's go in," said Lisa.

Looking at the display of colorful scarfs brought back a rush of memories surrounding that trip to the Hermès shop in London with her dad. She told Brendan the story and how she hoped she hadn't hurt her father's feelings the day he wanted to give her a gift that was important to him. So many years later, she still feared that she had.

"Would you like a Hermès scarf now for your birthday?" asked Brendan sweetly.

Avoiding the question, Lisa shook her head slightly. "You know, honey, I really do regret that I didn't pick out one of those scarfs when my father offered it." She paused to maintain her composure. Just the thought of her dear dad brought tears to her eyes. "You see, it was important to *him* . . ."

Pensively stroking one of the scarfs on the counter, she continued. "It was not *me* then, but it *is* me now. And if I'd known that my father was going to die two years later, that scarf from him would have been a treasure."

She fought to hold back tears as she squeezed Brendan's arm and guided their exit from the store.

She knew she hadn't answered Brendan's question, but she

didn't want to hurt *his* feelings too. In truth, unless the Hermès scarf came from Dad, it just wouldn't be the same.

The following evening Lisa and Brendan returned to their home on Martha's Vineyard. It was her actual birthday—and yes, it was her fiftieth. They picked up some mail and a small package that had come in their absence.

Lisa smiled as she recognized the writing on the package. It was from Aunt Nan, her dad's sister. Typically, her aunt had boldly written on the package "Do Not Open Until Your Birthday!"

What timing, Aunt Nan!

Lisa carried the package upstairs and sat on the bed. Brendan was still bringing things in from the car.

She tore open the top of the packing envelope. Slipped her hand inside . . . and felt it! She knew in an instant exactly what it was! It was soft. It was silky.

"Brendan!" she shouted with joy. "Can you come up here! Right away!"

Lisa started shaking. She closed her eyes . . . and took a long, deep breath. Tears began to fall. As Brendan rushed into the room, she finished opening the package.

"I know what it is!" she gasped, pulling out the most beautiful brown and gold Hermès scarf.

Aunt Nan's note explained that Lisa's father had bought

it for Lisa's grandmother. And now that Grandma was gone, Aunt Nan wanted Lisa to have the scarf.

"As Mother would always say, 'Wear it in good health,'" said Aunt Nan's note.

Lisa and Brendan were amazed by this gift from her father on her fiftieth birthday—and not even twenty-four hours after she and Brendan had talked about it.

This astonishing Godwink was a powerful *sign* from above, reaffirming the invisible connections between the natural world and the supernatural world, between where we live and where God—and Lisa's dad—live.

"I love my scarf," says Lisa. "And it's *me!*"

AFTERTHOUGHTS

God employs multiple ways to present you with Godwink *signs* of comfort and reassurance.

Often, as with Lisa, God uses inanimate objects to provide a special touch of love just when we need it most.

At other times—and this is what God did for Louise and me—His Godwink *signs* are both an inanimate object (the plot plan of the house) and the solution to the problem (the job Louise got out of the blue).

For Vin and Cesar, the *sign* was an object—the library card in the back of a book that tied together two people over a half a century—that confirmed for both of them that God is always present in each of our lives.

And to connect Karen Kingsbury to her dad, God used the inanimate object of a special song, but then to prove that He really was the One behind the song, God also divinely aligned Rod Stewart to be at the right place at the right moment. That Godwink *sign* was a beautiful gift at just the right moment.

God has Godwinks like these for you too!

And know that every time you receive a Godwink, God is reaffirming that He is omnipresent and that He personally cares about every aspect of your life.

And when you need a Godwink *sign*, pray. *Ask* for it, *believe* in His ability to deliver it, and *expect* to receive it.

WONDERS

Again and again in the ancient Scriptures, you will see God confirming His presence with signs and wonders. Your acknowledgment of the wonders He does in your life increases your ability to see them.

WONDER!

Words associated with wonder nearly always invite an exclamation point. Some examples are:

- Surprising!
- Awesome!
- Astonishing!

- Amazing!
- Marvelous!
- Miraculous!
- Phenomenal!

Godwink *wonders* usually leave us wide-eyed and open-mouthed. We are likely to exclaim—as the stories in this chapter illustrate—"Unbelievable!" or "Wow!" or to simply find ourselves speechless.

Secret #6 calls for us to acknowledge that God is the Source of all Godwinks of *wonder*. Through these *wonders*, God makes the clearest distinction between the natural world in which we live and the supernatural world where He exists.

As you read the following stories, please note the repeated challenge to wrap our human minds around things that we know simply cannot happen according to the laws of our physical world.

Rick LeClair: How to Stop a Twenty-Ton Rock

"You'll hear three blasts of a horn. The explosion will happen five minutes after that!" said Rick LeClair commandingly. It was a Saturday morning in May, and the muscular pastor, whose white hair and beard framed a kindly Santa-like face, was coaching the crowd that had gathered across the street from their church.

Rick knew what he was talking about. In between pastoring the church on Sundays and Wednesdays, he ran an earth-moving company. He was as comfortable in the seat of a bulldozer as he was riding his Harley or standing at his pulpit.

Glancing at the crowd of curiosity seekers, church members, and neighbors, Rick continued his warm-up talk with the verve of a football coach, even repeating himself for emphasis. "Those three blasts of the horn—one! . . . two! . . . three!— mean you have five minutes to clear the area. Next you'll hear two blasts of the horn. That means there's one minute to go." [1]

Rick scanned the faces etched with anticipation, then nodded to his sons, Dave and Eric, who were poised to take movies of the blast with their cell phones.

But neither Rick nor those gathered could have imagined what was about to happen.

Grace Ministries Church on Main Street in Saugus, Massachusetts, is cut into the bottom of a small hill, and its parking

---

1 Rick LeClair, personal interview by author SQuire Rushnell, May 14, 2014.

lot runs above and behind the building. The church had recently sold a piece of property adjacent to the parking lot for the construction of a charter school. Part of the arrangement was that Rick's company would do the site excavation.

For several days they prepared the land, digging down to the rock shelf that needed to be blasted. An explosives engineering company was brought in for that, and the detonation was scheduled for late Saturday morning when traffic was lightest.

Early that morning, Rick and his crew began the day with prayer as they always did. He asked for God's blessings on their tasks and for safety for all.

Rick was comfortable among people of all walks of life. His down-to-earth pastoral style had attracted a strong following of hardworking people to his Sunday morning services, while his Wednesday evening service was a motorcycle ministry for bikers.

"My husband is a good man and a very good pastor," says his wife, Ellen. "His Harley is his 'fishhook.' Men's lives change when they see him in his motorcycle jacket with a cross on the back. He leads 'em to a better life." [2]

---

2 Ellen LeClair, personal interview by author SQuire Rushnell, May 14, 2014.

On this Saturday morning Rick's fishhook was the blast of centuries-old rock to make way for development. He hoped to attract a crowd of people interested in seeing a rare event. If Rick could use this symbolism to spread some seeds about our need to stand on the rock of Jesus, he'd be using all of his God-given tools at the same time.

The moment had come. The people who had gathered tensed up when they heard the first three blasts of the horn.

Rick reviewed the procedure one more time: "Those first three blasts of the horn tell us we now have five minutes to go. Then, after the two blasts, we wait sixty seconds for the detonation!"

Some people in the crowd quipped nervously as the clock ticked.

The ominous final two shrieks of the horn pierced the quiet morning air, and the people braced themselves in anticipation of the explosion.

BAM!

The earth shook under their feet, as dirt and boulders rose from the hill above the church.

Then, in one voice, the crowd gasped as they saw the most incredible and frightening sight. A huge boulder—ten feet in diameter—rose into the air like a slow-motion rock-creature in an old horror movie. Then it rolled down the hill and across the parking lot—and it was heading directly toward the church!

"There goes our church," said Rick with understated dismay.

The giant runaway boulder rolled out of sight behind the church. Rick and the others froze for a moment, bracing themselves for the horror of seeing their church being smashed into a thousand pieces!

But . . . *nothing happened!*

Why is the building still standing? Rick wondered.

The crowd began to murmur as Rick led the way, slowly, cautiously, across the street and up the driveway to the back of the church.

They were stunned by what they saw! The massive twenty-ton boulder had inexplicably rolled to a stop just inches from the back wall of the church!

"Are you kidding me?"

"Oh my God!"

"Unbelievable!"

People could not believe their eyes.

"Don't get near it," warned Rick. He wasn't sure that the rock was sitting securely.

Still filming the event, David positioned the lens of the cell phone camera to show the gap between the boulder and the building.

"Six inches," said an off-camera voice.[3]

Panning down, David then showed the two-inch pipe railing around the back of the church. The railing had been completely squashed by the boulder.

"Maybe the railing stopped it," suggested a reporter from a local TV station.

Rick looked at the man and then back at the giant boulder.

"That rock came out of the ground like it was shot out of a cannon," Rick explained patiently. "It rolled down that hill with powerful force. That pipe railing was like a toothpick for that rock."

Rick paused before finishing.

"No. That rock was stopped by the hand of God."

What can we make of this?

Once again, God's *wonders* leave us wide-eyed and open-mouthed. We shake our heads in astonishment, unable to fathom what we have just witnessed.

Rick later talked about the miracle from a pastor's perspective. "The invisible is a world that exists. At this church we live by faith, and we see the invisible by faith. Today we saw God put up His hand and stop a twenty-ton rock! He kept that

---

3 David LeClair, https://www.youtube.com/watch?v=Uql3O3dGTOQ.

boulder from destroying a church that, through its food pantry, feeds two to three thousand people a month."

With the quiet wisdom of a pastor's wife, Ellen acknowledged that—along with his motorcycle jacket with the cross on it—her husband now had a new hook.

"For a long time to come, Rick will use the story of the rock as a fishhook to change men's lives," she said with a smile.

THE NATURAL WORLD VS. THE SUPERNATURAL

The reporter who watched the scene with only human eyes tried hard to find an explanation for the abrupt stop of the massive runaway boulder. A two-inch pipe would not have halted its downhill movement. What force could have? What power defied the laws of gravity and stopped the movement of that rock?

Secular media reporters are taught to dismiss God: He is not to be cited as the cause of or power behind anything. They are pressured by their peers to see events only through the lens of the natural world.

Rick, on the other hand, had the lens of the supernatural world, so he saw this amazing event as a Godwink of *wonder*. Rick knew that the boulder heading for the church, like an out-of-control locomotive, could only have been stopped by the hand of God.

THE WONDER OF ANGELS

Webster's dictionary defines *angel* like this: A spiritual being that serves as a messenger from God or as a guardian of human beings.

Angels must play a pretty important role in God's plan for all of us: they're mentioned over three hundred times in the Bible. Here's just one example:

> [*The* LORD] *will command his angels . . .*
> *to guard you in all your ways.*
> —PSALM 91:11 NIV

~~~

Tyler Beddoes: Angel of Spanish Fork

Some might think that twenty-nine-year-old Tyler Beddoes looked like the kid from *Leave It to Beaver* now grown up. This fit and trim officer had served on the Spanish Fork, Utah, police force for ten years.

It was a quiet Saturday morning in early March. Tyler checked the clock and then signed out of the police station. He was off to meet his wife, Brittany, and their three kids for a quick lunch at a nearby restaurant.

As Tyler drove to his destination just off Main Street, he couldn't help but feel pride and a touch of astonishment. Located just south of Provo, Spanish Fork had blossomed into a thriving community of forty thousand.

Brittany and the kids were already at Zupa's, the soup and salad place, when Tyler arrived. As he listened to the kids talk about their morning activities, his omnipresent police radio crackled with messages from the dispatcher.

Tyler was only halfway through his salad when he heard the report of an abandoned car under the Spanish Fork Bridge.

"This is six-jay-one-eight. I'll take it" was the follow-up

voice. Tyler recognized it: Bryan DeWitt was one of the other four officers on duty.[4]

"I better go," said Tyler, apologizing to Brittany and the kids. He was the officer-in-charge that day.

As he drove toward the bridge, a second report came over the radio. The fisherman who phoned in the first report had called back to say he saw a body in the car.

Tyler sounded the siren as he raced to Spanish Fork Bridge. Scrambling down the steep, rocky incline to the river below, he saw that Bryan had already gone into the cold, chest-high water. Tyler waded in next to him.

"It looks like there are two of them," said Tyler, peering into the squished, upside-down car, seeing a splay of female arms and legs.

He and Bryan flipped on their body cameras, newly issued to every policeman. Tyler later learned that his camera wasn't completely on and therefore didn't work.

They were joined by two other officers: Jared Warner also waded in, and Jason Harward maintained a position on the shore. Both men flipped on their body cams.

---

4 Ptolemy Tompkins and Tyler Beddoes, *Proof of Angels* (New York: Simon & Schuster/ Howard Books, 2016; Kindle Location 299; Howard Books, Kindle Edition).

The three working cameras recorded everything that followed.

Assessing the situation, the officers concluded that no one could have survived the accident. The roof of the car had been crushed inward. They began to move around the vehicle to determine what they should do.

Two minutes had passed since Bryan flipped on his camera.

Then they heard the voice. A high-pitched woman's voice.

Was that someone saying, "Help me, Help me!"? wondered Bryan.[5]

Each of the officers jumped into action.

Tyler heard the voice and Bryan's reply, "We're trying to get in there as soon as we can!"

"We're coming," said Jared, also responding to the woman's voice.

Now the team of officers, adrenaline pumping, lifted the three-thousand-pound car, filled with water, onto its side.

Tyler looked inside.

"Oh my God! There's a baby!"

Again there was a rush of adrenaline. A firefighter—one of several who had arrived on the scene—waded in alongside the

---

5 Pat Reavy, reporter, *Deseret News*, March 8, 2015.

police officers, reached in, and cut the child out of the seat. Then he handed her to Tyler.

Tyler saw her eyelids flutter.[6]

"There's life!" Tyler shouted, turning and handing the toddler to Jared, whose body camera recorded him moving as rapidly as possible toward the embankment, stepping carefully up the stones, and handing the child to the EMT standing next to the ambulance that had arrived. Jared then climbed in and accompanied the child to the hospital.

Tyler, Bryan, Jason, and the additional firefighters again dug deep to find the strength necessary to get the car fully upright. There remained in everyone's mind the nagging but unspoken notion that someone else must be in that car. Someone who was still alive. A woman. No one spoke about it, but that mysterious female voice raised questions in the minds of those three men.

The car was upright.

Now they could see inside. There was a young woman in the driver's seat—deceased—the only person in the car.

*   *   *

---

6 Tyler Beddoes, interview by author SQuire Rushnell, September 21, 2016.

Fourteen hours earlier, twenty-five-year-old Jenny Lynn Groesbeck was at her father's home south of Spanish Fork. She watched her dad firmly strap his eighteen-month-old granddaughter, Lily, into the car seat in the back.

Her darling daughter was so cute, dressed in a pink sweatshirt and a leopard-print jumpsuit.

Jenny then drove north on Main Street, a 45-mph zone, en route to her home in Springville, where she lived with Deven Trafny, Lily's father.

It is not known what happened next. But apparently, as Jenny approached Spanish Fork Bridge, where Main Street intersects with Arrowhead Trail on the left, her car suddenly veered to the right and through a space only inches wider than the car itself, the space between the bridge abutment and a group of trees. The car sailed through the air and then crashed upside down in the middle of the river below.

The shattered windshield let water rush in and submerge the young woman, but authorities later said she had died instantly when the top of the car was crushed inward.

There the car lay in a watery grave, invisible and unnoticed from the road until a little past noon the next day.

In the back, baby Lily hung upside down in her car seat, her face only inches from the cold forty-five-degree water that was flowing by.

When Tyler waded out of the Spanish Fork River, he discovered his wife, Brittany, waiting for him with a change of clothes. She smiled at him supportively. As he touched the back of his head, he discovered that he'd cut his head as well as his leg. So Bryan—joined by Jason and Tyler—climbed into an ambulance that rushed the three men to the hospital for treatment of injuries and hypothermia.

As they rode, they were quiet.

Tyler kept thinking, *Was I hearing things?*

About an hour and a half later, the four officers—the first responders—returned to the scene of the accident and began filing reports. Typically, they gathered together at the spot where an accident happened. Yet, very uncharacteristically, the four were not discussing the accident. Each one remained unusually quiet.

Tyler spoke first, and he spoke cautiously, not at all sure how his question would be received.

"When you guys were down there in the water . . . did you all hear a voice?"

For a moment the others said nothing.

"Yeah, I heard it," said Jason.

"Me too," said Bryan.

"So did I," said Jared.[7]

---

7 Tompkins and Beddoes, *Proof of Life*, Kindle location 378.

A few days later the foursome viewed the footage from the body cameras that Bryan, Jared, and Jason had worn. The audio on all three cameras unmistakably picked up a voice that spoke when the men were first in the water. A female voice was saying something to the officers. Although the words weren't clear on tape, each man definitely remembered hearing "Help me. Help me." The words were spoken not frantically, but in a calm, soothing manner.

Reinforcing the officers' belief that they had heard a voice was the further audio from the scene. Both Bryan and Jared could be heard replying to the voice with a sense of urgency. They were trying to get to whoever had just spoken to them and who must still have been alive in that car.

Each man could also attest that the feminine voice did not belong to one of them, nor to an unconscious baby in the back seat.

Some of those people who were directly involved that day concluded that the mysterious woman's voice was that of a supernatural angel whose purpose was to protect baby Lily.

POSTSCRIPT

"Little Lily is doing well," says her mother's sister, Jill Sanderson, eighteen months after the accident. "She's about to celebrate her third birthday."

It was Jill who practically lived at the hospital during the first touch-and-go days when Lily was in intensive care. Jill was the one given immediate temporary custody since Lily's father was away, working in Montana. Jill was bombarded by the media, and she did most of the sad work, like making the funeral arrangements for her sister and writing the obituary, all while keeping a vigil for Lily.

Though they were eight years apart, Jill and Jenny had been close.

"She was studying at Provo College—in the medical assistant program. She was attractive and well-liked," she said.

The sisters had grown closer after a family tragedy seven years earlier: their fifty-five-year-old mother, Karen, had died in a fire.

"She was a real angel," said a sobbing neighbor, explaining that Karen was an advocate for victims of domestic abuse.

After that tragic event the two sisters clung to each other. As they searched for meaning, they talked about their faith and about God.

"Jenny took Mom's death very hard," says Jill, "and she spent a lot of time at the cemetery."

But a common bond—that gave both sisters comfort—was the belief that "our mother was our guardian angel."

"We would buy each other angel trinkets. We talked of getting angel-wing tattoos. Jenny got two. I never got mine," Jill added sadly.

I asked Jill about the voice that the officers had heard at the scene of the accident.

"My first thought?" she asked. "I thought right away that the voice was my mother," she said.

> *Show hospitality to strangers, for thereby*
> *some have entertained angels unawares.*
> —HEBREWS 13:2

GOD AND HIS ANGELIC LITTLE MESSENGERS

For God to communicate with us through the innocence of a child is not all that unusual. Yet whenever it happens, we are almost always caught off guard and left to wonder.

Perhaps you too will be blessed with a sense of *wonder* when you see God working in the amazing story that follows.

~~~

Dechia Gerald: Words of Wonder from Wee Ones

3:45 a.m.

Matt Gerald rolled over, shut off the alarm, and started his daily routine. For people in law enforcement, Sunday mornings are no different from any other. An hour and a half later, he gave his beautiful wife, Dechia (Day-sha), a good-bye kiss.

"Love you, honey." [8]

She stirred but didn't awaken.

5:45 a.m.

Matt kidded and chatted with his fellow officers as they gathered for roll call at Baton Rouge Police Department. The handsome forty-one-year-old officer felt capable and confident: he was one year on the force, four months out of the academy, and this was his seventeenth day working on his own. He was well-liked and recognized as a good policeman as well as a good family man.

---

8 Dechia Gerald, interview with author SQuire Rushnell, October 28, 2016.

8:15 a.m.

Since Sunday mornings are normally slow, Matt and two fellow officers headed for coffee at the B-Quik convenience store a few blocks from the police station. Checking his watch, Matt thought he'd grab coffee and then text Dechia around the half hour, as usual.

8:30 a.m.

Dechia glanced at her phone. No text from Matt.

Her three-year-old daughter, Fynleigh, was still sleeping, and her older child, Dawclyn (Daw-slyn), was celebrating her ninth birthday with her dad in Alabama.

Sipping her coffee, Dechia glanced at the phone again. Still no text.

She had a bad feeling.

No real reason. She just did.

8:38 a.m.

At the B-Quik, one of the officers spotted a man outside, dressed in black, face covered, and carrying a rifle. The men quickly pulled their weapons, exited the store, and turned in the direction the man had been moving. Scanning the area, they carefully walked toward the rear of the building.

Hiding from view, the man with the rifle sneaked up from

behind and opened fire. Matt and the two others were ambushed: all three were fatally shot in the back.

8:45 a.m.

Dechia fidgeted. Still no text.

She flipped on the TV. Multiple police sirens were blaring in the background as a reporter revealed a shooting was in progress. Dechia recognized the location. It was B-Quik. She knew it from Matt's daily routine.

Her stomach turned.

She rapidly texted Matt.

"Hey, you OK?"

No response.

8:50 a.m.

Dechia needed information.

She texted a friend who had family members on the force. "Have you heard from your husband and brother?"

"Yes, they're OK."

8:55 a.m.

The phone began ringing. Family and friends were checking in to ask what she'd heard and how she was doing.

9:45 a.m.

There was a knock at the door. Five men were standing there with serious faces.

Dechia burst into tears.

"I knew . . . even before they told me. . . . I just knew," she said later.

10:00 a.m.

The house was filling up with people who had come to be with her, to pray with her and cry with her.

When Fynleigh, Dechia's little one, saw the house filled with confusion and everyone crying, she began to cry.

Adding to the craziness, reporters started knocking on the door, and their cars and vans began blocking the street.

Taking refuge in Dechia's lap, Fynleigh held her mother's face with both of her little hands and said, "Mommy, why are you crying?"

Dechia, forcing back tears, said, "Baby . . . Daddy has gone to be with Jesus."

They both cried.

10:30 a.m.

Dechia knew she had to tell her older daughter. She dialed Dawclyn's father in Alabama and told him what happened.

He was kind, sympathetic, and supportive. He said he would drive Dawclyn back to Baton Rouge. They discussed when she should be told.

"You can't drive eight hours without letting her know what's going on. It's best to tell her," Dechia finally decided.

Dawclyn was two years old when Dechia and Matt first met, and she was four when they were married. Now nine years old, she had grown to love her stepdad. She would take it hard.

Five days later, Friday

The morning of the funeral, Dechia was in her bedroom, feeling overwhelmed with grief, time pressure, and the stress of what to wear. Her mother and Dawclyn looked on.

"Everything I have seems snug!" Dechia snapped.

Sensing her mother's anguish, Dawclyn said with little-girl earnestness, "Mom, I don't know why you're fussing. You're going to have a baby."

"Dawclyn, you shouldn't say that." Dechia frowned, brushing away the nonsensical notion.

Three days later Dechia was bathing her three-year-old child.

Splashing her hands in the tub, Fynleigh seemed to be carrying on an imaginary conversation with someone.

"Who are you talking to?" asked Dechia.

"To Jesus about my baby brother in your tummy."

What? thought Dechia. *Both daughters talking about a pregnancy?*

Dechia's mind flashed to one morning, four years earlier. She was getting Dawclyn ready for school.

"Mommy's not feeling well today," she said offhandedly to her then five-year-old.

"Mom, you're not sick. You're going to have a baby," said the child matter-of-factly. "A girl."

"Who told you that?"

"Jesus. In my dream."

Dawclyn had been right! Nine months later Fynleigh was born.

With that kind of track record, Dechia decided to take no chances.

Later that day she picked up a pregnancy test kit at the pharmacy. She took the test as soon as she returned home. It was positive!

Days later doctors confirmed that Dechia was indeed having a baby; after several weeks more, they said it would be a boy—he was due in April.

It was bittersweet news.

"My dear husband left a very special gift behind . . ." She paused, gathering her thoughts and composure. "Honestly, there are days when I say, 'How am I going to do this?' But then . . . I feel a peace knowing that when I look into the eyes of that little baby boy, I'm going to see the eyes of Matt . . . and that is a gift from God."

Still, it was the innocent yet astonishing words from the lips of Dechia's children that leave us all with a sense of *wonder*, how God was using those two girls to deliver the news of a precious gift and peace of mind to Dechia—that out of the tragedy of her loss, He was providing her a treasure through Matt.

*Children are a gift from the L*ORD *. . .*
As arrows in the hand of a warrior . . .
How blessed is the man whose quiver is full of them!
—Psalm 127:3-5 ISV

Does God Protect Sacred Buildings?

St. Paul's Chapel is the oldest church in New York City. When it was built, a decade before the Revolutionary War, it was actually the city's tallest building. Of course, at that time, all of New York fit onto the tip of lower Manhattan.

When British troops captured the city, they set it afire.

One quarter of the buildings went up in flames. But St. Paul's Chapel, according to the newspaper of the day, "was unscathed," earning its nickname "the Little Chapel That Stood."

No one could have predicted how St. Paul's Chapel would again be tested 225 years later.[9]

By this time St. Paul's had become a popular tourist attraction. The rear of the church, facing Church Street, was across from the World Trade Center Towers. A large sycamore tree provided shade and rest for weary visitors, and inside the church, people loved to have photos taken at the very spot where George Washington had prayed on the day of his inauguration.

On September 11, 2001, terrorists forever changed America when they commandeered two passenger planes and flew them straight into the two World Trade Center Towers. These actions caused the buildings to collapse and took the lives of nearly three thousand men and women. When the towers fell, every building surrounding the World Trade Center was destroyed or severely damaged. Every building except for one.

Only one structure near ground zero remained unscathed,

---

9 Diana Aydin, "9/11 Miracle: The Little Chapel That Survived," *Guideposts*, September 9, 2015, https://www.guideposts.org/blog/9/11-miracle-the-little-chapel-that-survived, accessed October 20, 2016.

not even sustaining a broken window. That structure was St. Paul's Chapel. Once again it was "the Little Chapel That Stood."[10]

Anyone who stands at the rear of the chapel and looks across Church Street to where the World Trade Center once stood is amazed, overcome by *wonder* that the building remained standing—and undamaged.

For St. Paul's Chapel to be a Godwink of *wonder* twice in history is twice as amazing!

For nine months after 9/11, St. Paul's served as a shelter for hundreds of volunteers who were working twelve-hour shifts. St. Paul's served meals, provided beds, and offered prayer, comfort, and counsel to fire fighters, police, and construction workers.

The fence around the church became the primary spot for a sorrowful public to post impromptu memorials and photos of loved ones. Chapel officials originally thought that fifteen wooden panels attached to the fences would serve the needs of the people. They eventually provided four hundred panels.

Did God have something to do with protecting St. Paul's Chapel—a sacred property integrally tied to the birth of

---

10 Official Website of St. Paul's Chapel, part of Trinity Church of Wall Street, https://www.trinitywallstreet.org/about/stpaulschapel, accessed October 24, 2016.

America—not just once, but on two occasions when our country had been attacked by outside forces? We experience *wonder*. But how can we deny it?

⁓⁓⁓

Is the Bible Bulletproof?
Amazing Wonders in the News

Stories of events that defy natural laws rarely show up on national television, and when they do, the supernatural aspect is often downplayed.

The following stories *did* make the news, but mostly on local TV stations.

BIBLE SURVIVES BURNING VEHICLE
(WMC-TV, MEMPHIS, TENNESSEE)

Near Memphis, a reckless hit-and-run driver forced an unidentified man driving a Jeep off the highway.[11]

---

11 WMC TV, Memphis, TN, http://www.wmcactionnews5.com/story/31275611/exclusive-video-car-bursts-into-flames-on-385, accessed November 16, 2016.

The Jeep careened onto a center strip, struck a pole, and burst into flames.

Several other drivers quickly stopped to help. They ran to the burning car, broke a window, and pulled out the unconscious victim just before the vehicle was totally engulfed in flames.

Firefighters soon arrived and put out the fire as the man was rushed to the hospital.

The only thing left unharmed in the burned-out Jeep was the man's Bible. Sitting on the front seat. It didn't even appear singed.

"That is God," said Eugene McNeil, one of the rescuers, when he spoke with a reporter from WMC-TV. "If you don't believe it, I don't know what to say."

A police officer and another man who rescued the driver were so moved by the sight of the Bible, they stopped and prayed next to the smoldering car.

The men knew that God had saved the driver that night, and the Bible was a clear Godwink of *wonder*.

LADY ANTEBELLUM BUS FIRE
(NBC DFW, DALLAS, TEXAS)

When the tour bus for the country music band Lady Antebellum caught on fire, it destroyed everyone's personal belongings except for one item. And that item was singer Hillary Scott's Bible. She later told this to her audience:[12]

Everyone is safe and sound . . . [We are] thanking God for our safety and the safety of all of those who helped put this fire out.

Everything in the back of the bus was destroyed from the flames, except my Bible.

The outside cover was burned and messed up, but not one page was missing.

Y'all, God's Word will always stand.

My faith is forever deepened because of today.

I hope this story deepens yours.

Love you all!!!!

Hillary Scott

---

12 NBC DFW, Dallas, TX, http://www.nbcdfw.com/news/local/Bus-Fire-Blocks-I-30-in-Rowlett-Police-300079591.html, accessed November 16, 2016.

EXCEPT FOR THE BIBLE, EVERYTHING LOST IN HOUSE FIRE (WVLT-TV, NEWPORT, TENNESSEE)

Justin and Cynthia Wagner watched in horror: their two-story home was completely engulfed in flames.[13]

"Pretty much everything we own is gone," said Justin, sadly.

Sifting through the rubble the next day, they looked for anything that could have survived. It seemed hopeless.

"Look!" said Cynthia, reaching between charred rafters and soot. She pointed to the object. It was their Bible, unscathed and opened to a page that seemed to be a message directly from God. The Bible was open to John 3:16, showing a well-known verse that says:

For God so loved the world that
He gave his only begotten son,
that whosoever believes in him
shall not perish, but have eternal life.

---

13 WVLT, Newport, TN, http://www.local8now.com/home/headlines/Newport-loses
-everything-in-house-fire-364468041.html, accessed November 16, 2016.

"That verse tells you right there, that God is still here for us," said Justin.

BIBLE SURVIVES VEHICLE FIRE
(FOX10 NEWS, MOBILE, ALABAMA)

"The only thing that didn't burn was a Bible that I had," said Timothy Collier.[14]

Collier said that he and his wife were driving home when a gentleman passing in the opposite direction signaled him that his vehicle was on fire.

"Just after we got out, the car burst into flames," he said.

Yes, the family vehicle was totaled, but Collier truly believes a greater Power was watching over him and his wife.

"This Bible is the only thing that didn't burn," he said, shaking his head slightly. "The Bible made it through."

---

14 FOX10, Mobile, AL, July 9, 2015, http://www.fox10tv.com/story/29516566/bible
-survives-vehicle-engulfed-in-flames, accessed September 3, 2016.

*   *   *

In other stories on local television and radio stations across the country—extraordinary Godwinks of *wonder*—we hear about crosses that seemed to continually escape harm or, as in one case, prevented harm.

HUGE CROSS AVOIDS HARM,
BAFFLING FIREFIGHTERS
(CBN NEWS)

An iconic twelve-foot cross stands atop a mountain peak overlooking the San Gabriel Valley near Azusa, California, and it remained standing after flames ripped through the area. All seventeen hundred acres surrounding it were burnt and gone. The cross appeared to be lost, but the next morning, after the smoke cleared, the cross was still standing untouched.[15]

---

15 CBN News, September 7, 2014, http://www1.cbn.com/cbnnews/us/2014/January /Iconic-Cross-Still-Standing-after-Engulfed-by-Wildfire, accessed August 12, 2016.

CROSS SAVES WOMAN
(4 NEWS, COLUMBIA, SOUTH CAROLINA)

A grandmother was on her way to church when she was suddenly caught up in a raging flood. Out of nowhere a cross floated directly toward her. She grabbed hold of it and then clung to it for five hours until help arrived. That cross saved her life.[16]

CROSS RISES OUT OF THE RUBBLE OF 9/11
(*WASHINGTON POST*,
DISTRICT OF COLUMBIA)

Right after the 9/11 attack, Father Brian and other rescue workers gathered for a long moment of silence. They all were quiet before what Father Brian considered to be a Godwink *wonder*. Against seemingly insurmountable odds, a seventeen-foot-long cross of steel beams was raised up from the rubble. That rug-

---

16 Channel 4 News, Columbia, SC, http://kfor.com/2015/10/08/grandmother-holds-onto-churchs-cross-for-five-hours-to-survive-rushing-floods/, accessed August 12, 2016.

ged cross gave people hope during a horrific time in our country.[17]

IN SUM

If you're like me, the Godwink stories in this chapter feel like they are candidates for the *Ripley's Believe It or Not* books and attractions. Yet these accounts make a much larger point: whenever we exclaim words of *wonder*—amazing! wow! astonishing!—we may be simply awestruck by the Almighty! And when you acknowledge God's presence in the *wonders* around you, you have discovered another Secret—number 6— to getting more Godwinks and answered prayer.

---

17 *Washington Post*, https://www.washingtonpost.com/politics/911-memorials-the
-story-of-the-cross-at-ground-zero/2011/09/07/gIQA2mMXDK_story.html, accessed
August 12, 2016.

SECRET #7

DIVINE ALIGNMENT

---

*God divinely aligns us with other people
so that we are at exactly the right place at
exactly the right time, and He uses these
Godwinks in the unfolding of His plan.*

The fact is, you have been experiencing the *divine alignment* of Godwinks throughout your life. You just didn't know what to call it, or perhaps you didn't even recognize it.

Try this exercise.

Recall the circumstances and the people you encountered . . .

- just before you were offered a significant job or career opportunity.
- when you met someone who became very special to you.

Or when you made one of the following statements:

- "If I hadn't been at that place, at that exact moment, I wouldn't have learned about that job."
- "If I hadn't encountered so-and-so, I wouldn't have met the love of my life."

The aim of this chapter is to demonstrate how Secret #7—the *divine alignment* of Godwinks—has worked in people's lives so that you can better recognize the phenomenon as it happens in your own life, and even anticipate its happening.

The more *divinely aligned* Godwinks you learn to see, the more Godwinks and answered prayer you'll be thanking God for. And the better you'll comprehend the Godwink Effect.

You will have a growing appreciation and awareness for the ways in which God is actively involved in your life, often without your notice. You'll better comprehend that you have a built-in GPS—a God's Positioning System—that frequently *divinely aligns* you with the people and events He wants you to encounter so that He can get you where He wants you to go.

As He choreographs the miracles, blessings, and Godwinks He has for you, God also places unwitting messengers at specific spots at precise moments—people I call Godwink Links.

That's what happened to Mel Blanc, "the Man of a Thousand Voices."

First, come with me on a little background journey so that you can meet Mel Blanc, and some of his fascinating characters, as I met them.

Mel Blanc: Saved by the Bunny He Birthed

Joe Barbera, the affable creator and producer of some of America's favorite cartoons, such as *Tom and Jerry* and *The Flintstones*, was leading me through the back halls of Hanna Barbera Studios in Hollywood.

We were heading to the audio booth where Mel Blanc—the world's most famous voice-over artist of cartoon characters— was recording a script for a series that Joe, in association with the top-notch creative team Ruby-Spears, was developing for my ABC Saturday morning lineup. As vice president of ABC

Children's and Family Television, I had arrived from New York and couldn't wait to hear how the legendary Mel Blanc would breathe life into the star of one of my new shows for the network, *Captain Caveman.*

On paper, the character had grown very familiar to me: *Captain Caveman* was a Cro-Magnon superhero who exuded enthusiasm from a body buried in hair and who had one big flaw. He would sometimes lose his power and sputter down from the sky midflight.

But what did he *sound* like?

That was the question of greatest uncertainty for me. The voice and personality of a cartoon can make or break the series. Did he have a big booming voice or a small voice?

Peering through the glass window of the audio booth, I was instantly mesmerized. At the microphone, wearing a headset, sat the legendary Mel Blanc, making wild physical gestures and conjuring facial characteristics of our hero. Then I heard it for the first time: the unique voice of my new network star.

It was big! And it was gravelly! And it was perfect!

"Captain CAAAAAVEMAAAAAANNNN!"

I was tickled. Here was the man who had given birth to nearly every Warner Brothers cartoon character—from the hip, Brooklyn-sounding Bugs Bunny, "Eh, what's up, Doc?"

to Daffy Duck's "Yer despicable." From Sylvester's "Sufferin' succotash!" to Tweety Bird's "I tought I taw a puddy tat"—now giving life to a character that I had a hand in bringing to the kids of America!

Right then and there I had complete confidence that we would definitely have another hit on our hands in the fall when the *Captain Caveman* series premiered on ABC.

I have always loved stories about Mel Blanc.

His name was spelled *Blank* when he was growing up in Portland, Oregon. When he was young, he easily gained a reputation as the class clown. One day a teacher, frustrated with Mel's repertoire of voices, snapped sarcastically, "You're just like your name . . . *blank*."

Mel later pointed to that sarcastic remark as his prime reason for changing the spelling to *Blanc*.

On another occasion at school, Mel was strolling through an empty hallway and discovered that it had a unique echo. He couldn't resist letting loose a weird and wacky cackle that years later became the signature laugh of Woody Woodpecker. But on that day, he turned around and found himself face-to-face with the sourpuss school principal.

In the 1930s Mel Blanc went off to Los Angeles and rose to prominence in show business. Acknowledging that more voices emanated from Mel's larynx than anyone could imagine, comedian Jack Benny once said, "There are only five real people in Hollywood. Everybody else is Mel Blanc."[1]

But my favorite Mel Blanc story is one Joe Barbera loved to tell. It was when Mel did the voices of Barney Rubble and Dino for the hit animated series *The Flintstones* even though he was lying on a hospital gurney.

"Weeks before we were to record," said Joe, "Mel was in an auto accident so terrible they had to cut him out with a torch. Nobody thought he would live. He was in a coma for weeks. But then the most amazing thing happened." If Joe were here today, he'd call it a Godwink.

Mel's son Noel, then twenty-two, picks up the story. He rushed to his father's bedside at UCLA Medical Center to stand vigil with his mother, Estelle. Their state of shock grew heavier as the doctors' somber assessment began to sink in. His father's chances for survival, the doctors said, were one in one thousand.

"Dad was totally encased in a cast with nearly every bone in his body broken," says Noel. "He was in a coma, and they said the longer it lasted, the greater the likelihood of brain damage."

For the next two weeks, Noel and his mother took turns

---

1 *IMDB*, "Mel Blanc," Trivia, http://www.imdb.com/name/nm0000305/bio?ref_=nm_dyk_tm_sm#mini_bio.

pleading with Mel to speak, to emerge from the coma, and to show some sign of life.

"Dad! Dad! Can you hear me?"

"Mel, please wake up! Please come back to us."

On the fourteenth day of Mel's coma, a neurosurgeon was making his morning rounds. Dr. Louis Conway gazed down upon this mummy-like patient, quietly worrying that so much time had passed with Mel still in a coma. The doctor's head moved back and forth ever so slightly: should his famous patient survive, brain damage was almost a certainty.

In that moment, the doctor was distracted by something on the hospital TV screen. In the corner of his eye, he caught a familiar character swaggering across the screen. It was Mel's most famous bunny. (May I draw your attention to *divine alignment?*)

Offhandedly and quite uncharacteristically, Dr. Conway leaned over the bed and said something that, in the moment, felt silly.

"How are you feeling today, Bugs Bunny?"

From within the thick mass of bandages swathing Mel's head came a response: it was the unmistakable *voice* of Bugs Bunny![2]

---

2 Mel Blanc, http://deuceofclubs.com/books/252blanc.htm.

"Eh, just fine, Doc. How're you?"

Shocked, the doctor snapped to a standing position and looked over at the stunned faces of Noel and Estelle.

Dr. Conway leaned forward again. This time he said, "Porky Pig, how are *you* feeling?"

"J-uh-ju-uh-just f-fine, th-th-thanks!"

And then Mel himself started speaking, saying, "Where am I? What am I doing here?" and so on.

Several days later, as he reflected on what had happened, Dr. Conway found it quite profound. "I was astonished," he said. "Mel Blanc was dying, and it seemed as though Bugs Bunny was trying to save his life!"[3]

Mel's son Noel said the same thing, differently: "My dad breathed life into Bugs Bunny, and Bugs Bunny breathed life into him."

NYU neuroscientist Dr. Orrin Devinsky believes that Mel's brain injury was so severe that he may have lost his ability to interpret cues.

"Our brain constantly reacts to the cues it receives," he says.[4]

---

3 Dr. Louis Conway, http://www.radiolab.org/story/248590-blanc/.

4 Dr. Orrin Devinsky, http://www.radiolab.org/story/248590-blanc/.

Mel Blanc's entire life was a series of cues, prompting him to rapidly switch from one character to another, each of which was stored away in a different compartment of his brain. In essence, Mel's brain may have perceived Dr. Conway as the director, and the question "How are you feeling today, Bugs Bunny?" was his cue to reach into that other compartment and bring out Bugs.

What medical science can agree upon is that Mel began his recovery on the day that Bugs Bunny spoke through him. Even though Mel remained in a body cast for six more months, his family of characters went right back to work.

Joe Barbera said, "We set up a remote studio in Mel's bedroom. All the Flintstone voice artists gathered around his bed. Mel did Barney and Dino, and we recorded the tracks for sixty-five shows."

Mel eventually came back to near normal and continued to make cartoon voices for another thirty years. He lived to be eighty-one.

Noel picked up where his dad left off. Today he replicates his dad's cartoon voices closer than anybody else can.

The final words Mel recorded, just hours before he died, are the very words his family had chiseled on his headstone: Porky Pig's famous sign-off, "That's all, folks!"

Dr. Conway was an unwitting messenger—a Godwink

Link—sent into Mel's hospital room by an unseen force at the precise time that Bugs Bunny would be appearing on TV, to accomplish God's plan to heal Mel—in a manner that was unheard-of—and give him another thirty years of life on earth.

Was it by coincidence that the doctor was at Mel's bedside just as Bugs Bunny swaggered across the TV screen? Was it mere chance that the doctor, very uncharacteristically, felt prompted to ask, "How are you feeling today, Bugs Bunny?"

No, it was the *divine alignment* of Godwinks.

When Dr. Conway spoke those words—an offhand comment—God's supernatural power released instantly; Mel's brain rebooted, and everything fell into perfect order.

Here's a comforting thought for each of us: God will also *divinely align* you with the right people as He works out His plans for you. God may also use you as a Godwink Link to unwittingly carry a Godwink to someone else—the same way God used Dr. Conway in Mel Blanc's life.

DOING AN ARCHEOLOGICAL DIG INTO YOUR PAST

During the two decades I was working at ABC with Mel Blanc and Joe Barbera, other Godwinks happened, yet by and large

I was oblivious. I hadn't yet learned to recognize them. I've since discovered that many Godwinks in our personal history are unearthed only when we do an archeological dig into our own pasts, revisiting key moments with people we encountered along the paths we traveled, moments that often resulted in unexpected blessings.

Once you do that search, it's likely you'll begin to see Godwinks and *divine alignment* at every crossroad of your life.

With hindsight, I discovered many occasions when I "just happened" to be at the right place at the right time for God to wink and to *divinely align* me with people or paths He wanted me to meet or to take. It was exciting to rediscover Godwinks that had never fully registered at the time or which I had shrugged off as interesting but not relevant.

I'm betting the same will happen to you; an archeological dig into your own history may produce some extraordinary Godwinks that you've already experienced.

The following Godwink story is now one of my favorites.

Godwinks and Schoolhouse Rock

At speaking engagements I'm often introduced as a former ABC executive and *one* of the fathers of *Schoolhouse Rock*. I emphasize *one* because success usually has many fathers.

Still, the endurance of that series never fails to astonish me: a series of three-and-a-half-minute musical cartoons that aired on our ABC Saturday morning schedule forty years ago and which can still be sung by millions of baby boomers and kids today. You cannot imagine how many people have said that *Schoolhouse Rock* helped them through math, English, or history.

Among the twenty-eight programs that aired during the seventies and eighties, "Conjunction Junction" is unquestionably the all-time most popular. A portly train conductor directs colorful boxcars over crisscrossing railroad tracks to a catchy tune "Hookin' up words, and phrases, and all kinds of things." In your memory, can you go back to moments in childhood when you stood in front of the TV, singing along as that conductor scampered to the top of a caboose?

The second most popular episode was "I'm Just a Bill," featuring Jack Sheldon's gravelly voice and the writing of David

Frishberg about a little bill trying to make it through Congress. It amused me to later understand why "I'm Just a Bill" was so frequently requested by Washington lobbying groups. In three and a half minutes they could teach their staffs what it takes for a bill to go through Congress!

Now for the backstory on *Schoolhouse Rock*. As with many things when you look back on them, it never would have been birthed without the *divine alignment* of Godwinks.

In the early seventies, a woman with political savvy outside Boston, Peggy Charren, led an activist group of mothers who called themselves Action for Children's Television (ACT). These mothers were quite successful in their first goal: to attract the attention—and perhaps the ire—of network television executives.

They did this by taking their complaints not to the networks but directly to Congress. They argued that the television networks should be required to increase their "pro-social" and educational programming for children and decrease the number of advertisements for food products devoid of nutrition. With several influential congressmen on their side, ACT garnered a good amount of press and agitated a good number of broadcast executives.

Michael Eisner, head of ABC Daytime and Children's Programming, was meeting with his ad agency, McCaffrey

McCall.[5] As their discussion about advertising wrapped up, David McCall, president of the firm, casually mentioned to Michael that his son was having difficulty learning the multiplication tables. (Please see the *divine alignment* here.)

He suggested that perhaps ABC could produce some short programs that would teach kids the fundamentals of math. Soft-spoken Tom Yohe, the agency's creative head, said they had been working on an idea called *Multiplication Rock*, and he began to sing "Three's a Magic Number."

What David and Tom didn't know was that, for Michael, the number three was significant (more *divine alignment*). He later told me, "Although I'm Jewish, I went to a mostly Christian grade school, an Episcopal high school, and a Baptist college. I therefore understood the 'magic' of the number three and the 'magic' of the Trinity."[6]

Michael also knew that in most religions the number three represents *connection* between past, present, and future.

As Yohe sang, Michael thought the folk-jazz tune was catchy and liked its educational aspects, especially since Action for Children's Television was clamoring for better children's programming (*divine alignment*).

---

5 Michael Eisner, interviewed by author SQuire Rushnell, August 1, 2016.

6 Michael Eisner, ibid.

Right there on the spot, somewhat to the surprise of McCall and Yohe, Michael decided to include the programs in the Saturday morning lineup that he was currently preparing to present at the upcoming ABC Affiliate Meeting, the network's most significant annual meeting (*divine alignment*, again).

A few weeks later Michael stood before the gathering of affiliates. He explained that in between new full-length Saturday morning cartoons, ABC would schedule three-and-a-half-minute entertaining and educational programs called *Multiplication Rock*.

The affiliates were delighted that their network was doing something to lessen the heat from the mothers of ACT—and something so clever at that!

McCaffrey McCall quickly put their top creative people to work on the series.

Tom Yohe employed his own artistic talents to design *Multiplication Rock*'s distinctive look and characters. George Newall, another member of the creative team, had an exceptional knowledge of music. He was the one who had approached Bob Dorough, a jazz musician he'd known (more *divine alignment*), to write some songs, including "Three's a Magic Number."

Bob was now hired to write all eleven programs that would teach the multiplication tables—among them "My Hero Zero," "Naughty Number Nine," and "Little Twelvetoes"—

while Yohe and Newall served as producers under the agency's new Scholastic Productions division.

The following season Michael Eisner moved on to head up ABC prime-time television, triggering subsequent changes that led to my role as vice president for ABC Children's Television. Eisner remained at ABC a few seasons longer before being lured to Paramount as president and then to his most noted role, CEO of Disney.

I made it a priority in my new job to set a meeting with Tom Yohe and George Newall. I told my staff of this Godwink: Tom Yohe and I had already met. He had been a couple of years ahead of me at Syracuse University, and we were fraternity brothers (can we say *divine alignment?*).

Still, as Tom and George approached that first meeting, I can only assume they felt some apprehension. Would I, the new guy in charge, carry on what Michael Eisner had started? Or—as network executives sometimes do—would I want to go in another direction?

I was definitely not going to change direction. It was clear to me that *Multiplication Rock* played an important role in the ABC schedule not only as a creative asset, but also in terms of the public's awareness that we were indeed addressing concerns raised by Action for Children's Television.

George and Tom suggested that they could create additional programs for other elementary school subjects like English, history, and science. They shared some of their ideas.

Musing on that, I said, "Well . . . we certainly can't call it *Multiplication Rock* any longer."

My mind drifted to the name of their production division—Scholastic—and I offered, "Why not call it *Schoolhouse Rock*?"

So, as simple as that, my offhanded comment provided the series with a name that stuck. And who would have thought that more than four decades later an entire segment of the population would feel a deep fondness for—almost an *ownership* of—the *Schoolhouse Rock* programs? I can think of no other program in the history of television that elicits a similar response.

Over the next decade *Schoolhouse Rock* blossomed. Bob Dorough wrote more songs, including "Conjunction Junction" and the singable "Lolly, Lolly, Lolly, Get Your Adverbs Here."

Other people emerged to play significant roles in the evolution of *Schoolhouse Rock*. Rad Stone was the agency's account executive who oversaw all the business matters with ABC; Lynn Ahrens, an assistant at the agency, submitted some ideas, and several of her songs—including "Preamble" and "Interjections"—became *Schoolhouse Rock* favorites. She was the second most prolific writer of *Schoolhouse Rock* songs and later went on to write such Tony Award–winning Broadway shows as *Ragtime*.

So, by digging into my own history with *Schoolhouse Rock,* I now clearly saw the fine threads of *divine alignment*. Godwinks had been knitted together one by one. Were it not for the displeasure of some Boston mothers, an ad executive's son's frustration with math, and the programming pressure felt by network executives, *Schoolhouse Rock* might never have happened.

Clearly, *Schoolhouse Rock* did not come about randomly or by accident. God had planned every piece to fit together perfectly in order to accomplish the result that He wanted.

Forty years after the first airing, I find nothing more rewarding than seeing the Godwink Effect of *Schoolhouse Rock* rippling across time, from generation to generation.

THE MULTIPLICATION OF GODWINKS

When you open your mind to the immense possibilities of *divine alignment*, you can begin to see how God is constantly connecting you with one person and then another, keeping you on the course *He* wants you to take. You will also see that you have been experiencing the multiplication of Godwinks more than you knew.

That happened to Roma Downey, the wonderful actress who played the lead angel on the television series *Touched by an Angel*. Looking back over her life, she saw how God had *divinely aligned* her path so that she would be at exactly the right place, at the right time, to bring hope and light to a young woman in desperate circumstances.

Roma Downey: An Angel on Earth

The young woman approached Roma with a look of timid determination.

It was common for people to recognize Roma. After all, her television series took her into twenty million homes every week.

"I want you to know that you helped save my life," said the young woman, her voice shaking slightly.[7]

"How was that?" asked Roma sweetly.

---

7 Roma Downey, interview with author SQuire Rushnell, January 30, 2012.

The woman raised her wrists for Roma to see her pale skin reddened around fresh scars.

"I . . . I was taking my own life," she said, hesitantly. "I felt abandoned . . . by my family and by God. My blood was spilling onto the bathroom floor, my back was to the wall, I was sliding down, collapsing, waiting to die.

"In my final desperate cry to God, I screamed, 'Even now there is no word from You, God, because You are not there!' "

The frail young woman's eyes widened as she looked directly at Roma.

"But His reply came . . . from *you!*" she said.

Now Roma's eyes widened.

"You said, 'You are *not* alone. You have never been alone. Don't you know that God loves you?' "

Roma was puzzled. *What does this young woman mean?*

Silent, the two women looked searchingly into each other's eyes. Then the young woman swallowed, holding back her tears.

"It was you," continued the young woman. "In answer to my plea for God to show Himself to me—and as I sat in a puddle of my own blood—I heard *your* voice!"

In a surreal millisecond Roma now realized the Godwink that had occurred: God had *divinely aligned* her voice on an episode of *Touched by an Angel* to be a lifeline for this poor woman at the precise moment of her greatest desperation. From the TV in another room, this precious young woman had heard the phrase that was written into every show—the production crew called it "the angel revelation scene"—when the actor who played an angel revealed their identity to someone in trouble.

Momentarily frozen in astonishment at the unbelievable odds against the unfolding of this amazing, *divinely aligned* Godwink—after all, thousands of hours of television programs and millions and millions of words are broadcast every day—Roma refocused on the young woman as she continued her story.

"I wrapped my wrists in a towel and called for an ambulance," she said with a sigh. "*That* is how you saved my life."

Roma looked at her with compassion and managed an astonished, whispered response. "And *that* is evidence that angels on earth are messengers for an ever-present God."

With each of them choking back tears, Roma wrapped both arms around the young woman and held her for a long moment.

They felt a profound peace as they sensed God's love shining exclusively on the two of them. Ever so tenderly, He had stitched together their lives with the invisible threads of *divine alignment* and the Godwink effect.

Roma is correct: there indeed are angels on earth who are messengers of God. We have another name for them. We call them teachers. You'll see what I mean in this final illustration of *divine alignment*.

May the LORD be praised,
for He has wonderfully shown His faithful love to me . . .
In my alarm I had said,
"I am cut off from Your sight."
But You heard the sound of my pleading
when I cried to You for help.
—PSALM 31:21-22

Cindy and Katelynn:
A Divinely Aligned Wink of Life

It was after eight a.m. on a mid-September morning, just a few days into the new school year.

Substitute teacher Cindy Santos slid behind the wheel of her car and began the ten-minute drive from her Blandon home in central Pennsylvania to Richmond Elementary School.

Cindy liked subbing. The scheduling flexibility fit the needs of her busy household with her husband, Matt, and three boys, aged thirteen to eighteen. She also enjoyed the variety of going from class to class, from school to school.

Driving familiar back roads, flanked by picturesque farmlands with neat rows of dry corn, she considered that today—her first assignment of the year—would be both a treat and a challenge. Overseeing a class of cute kindergarteners ought to be fun.

Then she had second thoughts: this was an unusually large class—twenty-seven kids. *This may be pretty tough,* she thought with a sigh. *Many of those children, unaccustomed to school, will still be missing their moms and dads.*

As she does several times a day, Cindy said a prayer.

I'm relying on You for guidance today, God!

As it turned out, this would be the *only* time in the entire school year that Cindy would oversee a kindergarten class. But it would be her most amazingly auspicious school day ever!

And one of our most heartfelt examples of the divine alignment of Godwinks.

Elsewhere in central Pennsylvania, Chris and Alicia Ernst's household was bustling with morning activity. Their older daughter, eleven-year-old Kayla, caught her bus to middle school around 8:00. With the help of eight-year-old Kameryn, Alicia was readying five-year-old Katelynn for the 8:45 bus to Richmond Elementary. Kameryn relished the role of being Katelynn's big sister ever since Katelynn got sick. Every day she watched out for Katelynn all the way to school and all the way home.

Alicia, who had given birth to her fourth child a year earlier—a little boy, Noah—had a definite routine as she dressed Katelynn. She carefully folded the twelve-inch tube into a horseshoe shape, bandaged it to Katelynn's tummy, secured the open end of the tube with tape, and hid it under her child's top. It was through this tube that Katelynn received dialysis for her kidney failure from 8:00 p.m. to 6:00 a.m. every night. The only interruption would be if the machine acted up during the night and Alicia had to get up, clean it, and reactivate it. Such an occurrence would extend Katelynn's treatment into the morning, for she needed to complete the required ten hours a day of dialysis.

Chris had to allow a half hour for his drive to work, arriving at the bank by 9:00 a.m. This daily commute was quiet time for him, one of the very few times during the day that he was totally alone. At home, he was dad, husband, breadwinner, and Mr. Steady Hand.

"He is my rock," Alicia is fond of saying. "I'm a wreck, but he's the strong one."

But when he was alone in the car, Chris didn't have to maintain his optimistic attitude. He had thirty minutes to sort through matters of concern—the mounting medical bills, his constant worry that Katelynn had a death sentence hanging over her head, and his frustration that Alicia and he were still desperately trying to find a kidney donor for their little girl.

Alone in his car Chris could cry out to God and even rail at Him when he saw other children who had started treatment at the same time that Katelynn did but were already being healed of kidney failure. Or when he learned that people who had answered his Facebook plea for a kidney donor for his daughter later said they had contacted the hospital and never heard back.

"Shouldn't they have more people answering the phone?" he privately shared with Alicia.

Lately his faith was beginning to fade. From behind the steering wheel, Chris shouted, "Where *are* You in all this, God?"

Before walking into the classroom at Richmond School, Cindy Santos had a short chat with the school nurse, Doreen, a friend, who told her that one little girl in her class would need special attention.

There she was. Petite auburn-haired Katelynn Ernst with sleepy brown eyes.

She's so cute! Who could not love that child? thought Cindy, feeling an instant compassion for Katelynn.

According to the nurse, Katelynn had been awaiting a kidney transplant for many months, was on dialysis ten hours a day, and took twelve daily medications. She was quieter than the other children, but Cindy was definitely drawn to her.

Cindy's day with the kindergartners came and went. The next day she was on to another classroom at another school. Yet occasionally floating through Cindy's mind, despite the hubbub of life, was the image of little Katelynn.

Ten days later, a Godwink happened.

Cindy was scrolling through the Facebook page of a friend when an image labeled "Katelynn's Kidney Journey" somehow popped up in the right-hand column. (*Divine alignment?*)

I wonder if this is the same Katelynn, thought Cindy, clicking the icon.

There she was! The same little girl with those remarkably engaging eyes and, in this picture, a slight smile. Cindy read with interest the heartfelt notes of well-wishers, all hoping that

Katelynn would soon find a kidney donor. Her parents had written about the difficulty of locating a perfect match. Everyone in Katelynn's family and many family friends had been scratched off the list of possible donors.

Cindy read the initial requirements: compatible blood type, A or O; good health; age between eighteen and seventy.

Hmm . . . I could be a fit, thought Cindy.

She saw a telephone number to call for more information. She stared at it a moment . . . and then logged off Facebook.

The following day Cindy decided to talk with her husband, Matt, about meeting Katelynn. They talked about how hard it must be for her parents to let go and send their sick child to school, and how concerned they must be for her. Cindy also admitted to Matt that the little girl had remained on her mind.

"How would you feel about me calling that number and exploring the matter further?" she asked gently.

Understanding his wife's curiosity, Matt said it couldn't hurt to get more information.

The next day Cindy reached for the phone, dialed the number, and was soon talking with a charming person named Vicky, who was the transplant coordinator at Hershey Children's Hospital. Vicky provided extensive details about what was involved and some of the risks. Then she promised to send Cindy a packet of information explaining that if the initial blood tests didn't rule her out, Cindy would be asked if she was willing to undergo a full day of testing at Hershey Children's Hospital, an eighty-minute drive away. Finally, Vicky cautioned that there was an 80 percent likelihood that Cindy would not meet the donor requirements.

She decided to take one more step forward.

Confiding to no one other than her husband and still unsure about being a donor, Cindy nevertheless continued to feel that exploring the matter until she had all the necessary information was the right thing to do. It wasn't long before she received notice that her full day of testing was scheduled for October twenty-fifth.

The night before her appointment, Cindy drove to Hershey and stayed at a nearby hotel so she could be at the hospital at the crack of dawn.

Before going to bed, Cindy wanted to be sure that she was doing what God wanted her to do. She prayed for protection over her husband and her children, and she prayed for the Ernst family.

As she thought about Katelynn and her family, Cindy acknowledged that she was about to take a bold step of faith and realized that the Ernsts knew nothing about this. There was no way for them to know what Cindy was doing: it was against hospital policy to share patient information.

Those parents must be so worried for their little girl, Cindy thought as she opened up her computer. Locating the family's Facebook page, she clicked the message icon, and this is what she wrote:

> I wanted to send you a message to introduce myself
> since tomorrow I am heading to Hershey Med Center
> for a full day of tests and meetings to possibly become
> Katelynn's living donor.

Alicia and Chris were out shopping when Alicia's phone dinged that she had a message. She clicked the Facebook notifier, whooped out loud, and then excitedly read the message to Chris. It ended with:

> I'm Cindy Santos, and I met Katelynn in school. I was
> a substitute teacher in her class.

Alicia and Chris hugged each other long and hard in the aisle of the store.

At the end of her day of testing, Cindy was told that the results would take about four weeks to evaluate. They would let her know the outcome at the end of November.

Five days after her trip to Hershey, on October thirtieth,

Cindy had another Godwink. She was back at Richmond Elementary School, not as a teacher this time but to serve as a teacher's aide in various classes. She smiled inwardly when she saw that one of the classes where she was scheduled to spend thirty minutes was kindergarten. And one of the four children she would work with was Katelynn Ernst. (Wow . . . more *divine alignment* of Godwinks!)

As she held flash cards for her darling little friend, Cindy couldn't help thinking about the Godwinks that were popping up. *Of all the kids in this school, here I am sitting with Katelynn, and she has no clue that just days ago, I went through massive testing to possibly save her life.*

She reminded herself that she had not yet fully come to terms with the "what ifs":

What if they find that I am *qualified? What if I am the twenty-percent chance for candidacy? What will I do? Will I say yes?*

Cindy couldn't help but think that the series of Godwinks were God's means of encouraging her. Then, in a moment of sober thought, she asked herself, *Am I following God's plan . . . or is this my own plan?*

Cindy's session with Katelynn was suddenly interrupted.

Another teacher's aide rushed in and said to Cindy, in a low voice, that she needed to escort Katelynn to the principal's office; her mother was there to pick her up.

With a whispered aside, the teacher added buoyantly, "They're rushing her to Hershey Children's Hospital. They've found a kidney donor for Katelynn!"

Cindy watched as her little friend was ushered out of the classroom.

Well, God, maybe this is a sign. And if You have another way to save this child, hallelujah!

But as Cindy went on to her other classes, she found herself needing to sweep away the little question that kept creeping into her consciousness: *Am I disappointed that the donor isn't me?*

Alicia Ernst received the call from Hershey that they had a deceased donor and that the kidney was a match, so please get to the hospital as soon as possible! Alicia ran to the car and telephoned Chris as she drove to pick up Katelynn at school. He said he'd leave right away and meet them back at the house.

"Katelynn didn't know what was going on," said Alicia. "After all, she was only five. When I picked her up from school, she seemed so frail. She was always exhausted after the dialysis every night. Still, we needed to get her to the hospital as quickly as possible."

The medical team in Hershey quickly prepped Katelynn, giving Alicia and Chris a few moments to step into the hall, where they could pray. Down the hallway they saw a family gathered, crying together. Alicia and Chris knew they had lost a child.

"God, please be with them," said Alicia, "and with us."

When Alicia and Chris returned to the room, they were cautiously hopeful that in just minutes Katelynn would be given a new kidney, a new lease on life.

As nurses were hooking up Katelynn's IV, the phone rang. It was the operating room. The doctor wanted to speak to both parents.

"I'm sorry," he said. "The kidney from the deceased donor is not functioning properly. We cannot do the transplant."

Hopes were dashed, yet again.

Alicia began to sob, and Chris squeezed his lips together to keep from crying.

"God has a plan," said Alicia, her voice breaking. "I just know He has a plan."

"We have to keep believing that," counseled Chris. "Let's remember that Katelynn's teacher was tested. Maybe *she's* the one."

In his mind he asked himself, *Do I really believe that? It's such a struggle to believe anymore.*

* * *

Cindy felt she needed information. Later that day she decided to check Katelynn's Kidney Journey on Facebook to see if anything was there.

Her heart sank. She read that Katelynn had not received the transplant.

She felt so sorry that the Ernst family's hopes were once again raised and then shattered.

Suddenly, Cindy felt a little worried. *What if I don't qualify to be her donor? How much can that child—and her parents—bear?*

Even though Cindy was waiting patiently to receive a call from Vicky at Hershey Children's Hospital, she was surprised when the call arrived the day after Thanksgiving.

Vicky was speaking excitedly: "You have been approved to be Katelynn's kidney donor!"

Cindy felt a huge rush of emotion. She was glad she was now in a position to say yes—to save Katelynn's life—but face-to-face with the decision, *Will I?*

Vicky continued on with the report. She said Cindy's day-long testing had turned up something unusual—she had a rare medical condition called pelvic congestive condition.

"Oh my," said Cindy. "I've had severe stomach pain on

occasion. But the pain would subside, so I've never bothered to get it checked."

"Well," said Vicky, "the doctors evaluating your case called in a specialist, an ob-gyn, to ask if that condition would disqualify you as a donor. They were told that, on the contrary, the removal of one of your kidneys would relieve the pressure on the pelvis and thereby forestall certain surgery for you in the future."

Wow! Another Godwink! Cindy was having a hard time counting all of them.

Do I really need any more divinely aligned nudges before I step out in faith and agree to be Katelynn's donor? Cindy asked herself.

Vicky continued, "This type of surgery is done on Tuesdays, and we can schedule you and Katelynn for December seventeenth. What do you think?"

Cindy hesitated.

There was a moment of noticeable dead air.

"Well . . . do you think we could try to have it scheduled earlier?" asked Cindy. "That way Katelynn and I could both be home for Christmas."

Vicky agreed to try.

She called back a short while later and asked, "Will December tenth work for you?"

"Yes!" said Cindy.

With only about two weeks to go before the surgery, Cindy still felt a small disconnect because she hadn't yet met Katelynn's parents. Then, six days before the procedure, Cindy was asked to go to the hospital for pre-admission testing.

"Katelynn and her parents will be there on the same day for Katelynn's pre-admission," said the administrator, "but we don't know what time."

A friend of Cindy's volunteered to drive her to the hospital. The friend's mom lived in Hershey, so while Cindy was doing what she had to do, the friend would visit her mom and then swing back to pick up Cindy.

Alicia and Chris had also been told that Cindy would be on the premises, but it was not known when.

"There she is," said Alicia excitedly, recognizing Cindy from her Facebook photos as Chris drove into the hospital parking lot. "She's standing right there at the curb!" (More and more *divine alignment*.)

Chris pulled over. The three jumped out of the car, ran toward Cindy, and introduced themselves. The adults shared a group hug. Then, when Cindy got down to her level, Katelynn's hug was the warmest of all.

It was during that small chat that yet another Godwink was revealed. They discovered that they had also been *divinely aligned* geographically. Both families live in Blandon, Pennsylvania, and their homes are within walking distance!

On the evening of December ninth, Cindy's parents stayed overnight with the boys while Matt and Cindy drove to Hershey. They had made reservations at the same hotel Cindy had stayed at for her day of testing. And that was the setting for one more Godwink . . . a confirmation that God was right there next to them. When they walked into their room, Cindy realized it was the very room she had stayed in before.

It was still dark when Cindy and Matt arrived at the hospital the next morning. Her prep was scheduled for six a.m. They were told that Cindy would go into surgery first and have her kidney removed.

As Cindy lay on the hospital gurney, she began to shiver. It was cool in the room, and she was wearing only a hospital gown. But she knew that her shaking was not because she was cold. Her anxiety was peaking.

"I was so nervous. I had to keep praying, *Please, God! Give me the strength I need.*"

She tried to sort out her feelings. She hadn't even been this nervous when her boys were born! *Why am I so scared now, God?*

She realized that during childbirth she was concerned only

about herself and her baby. But in this situation, so much more was at stake. She began to think of all the risks that Vicky had been required to tell her, as part of the hospital's full disclosure. Those risks were now spelled out in her mind in neon letters.

I'm now taking risks with the mother of my children . . . and the wife of my husband. My risks also affect the life of a sweet five-year-old girl . . . and her parents . . . her sisters and her brother.

Cindy continued to shake. A nurse brought her a warm blanket.

Then Cindy thought about the deacons at her church. The pastor had asked them to pray for her as she approached this big day. One deacon gave Cindy a verse from the Bible, Deuteronomy 31:8, and Cindy memorized it. Lying on the gurney, she began to recite it:

> *The LORD himself goes before you*
> *and will be with you;*
> *he will never leave you nor forsake you.*
> *Do not be afraid; do not be discouraged.*

Soon a peace and comfort washed over her. She stopped shaking.

A short while later Cindy went into surgery to have one of her kidneys removed. Katelynn would follow and receive the gift of life. Or more specifically, the gift of a lifetime from a substitute teacher who had been *divinely aligned* into her classroom for one day only.

From that day forward, Cindy Santos played a large role in Katelynn's Kidney Journey. The two—as well as Alicia and Chris—can see a trail of amazing Godwinks that *divinely aligned* their paths for this very purpose.

Cindy and Katelynn see each other occasionally throughout the year. But there are two dates that they never miss celebrating: Katelynn's birthday, August twentieth, and her "kidney-versary," December tenth.

"Everything played out like Cindy was sent from heaven," says Katelynn's mom. "She's an angel."

"No, I'm not," insists Cindy. "But I do believe I was put into Katelynn's classroom not by coincidence but by divine intervention."

"We feel exactly the same way," says Alicia. "God sent Cindy to us."

"It makes you appreciate life," adds Chris. "This experience has strengthened our faith and brought my wife and me closer together."

Katelynn now leads a normal life. She is active, happy, and

healthy. And the screensaver on her telephone is a darling picture of Cindy and her.

Understanding the Godwink Effect means seeing and gathering the invisible threads that connect your Godwinks dot by dot. God uses Godwinks to cause you to be exactly where He wants you to be and to encounter exactly whom He wants you to encounter. When you recognize Godwinks, you can piece together the tapestry of your life that is being woven right before your eyes! And that is the principle of Secret #7, *Divine Alignment*.

SUMMARY

At the beginning of this book we said:

As a child you were fascinated to learn that a pebble tossed into a pond will cause multiple ripples upon the water.

The Godwink Effect is the series of ripples that result from Godwinks dropping wondrously into your life. . . .

While it is special and comforting to think of every Godwink as an exclusive communication directly from God to you, out of seven billion people on the planet, God's blessings usually have more than one purpose or person in mind. Therefore, an initial Godwink frequently results in multiple outcomes, even producing a cascade of Godwinks that can lift you and many others.

We are hopeful that this book has provided you with a fresh perspective from which to evaluate the Godwinks that occur to you.

Further, we trust that the Seven Secrets discussed here will help you develop a keen awareness and "eyes to see" the God-winks and answered prayers that you experience day in and day out.

ONCE AGAIN, THE SEVEN SECRETS

Secret #1: PRAY

Godwinks and prayer are inextricably linked. When you **pray** more, you experience more Godwinks. The best prayer is intentional, but God occasionally proves He can hear your heart by answering unintentional or even unasked prayers. When you pray with a partner, Godwinks and answered prayer increase.

Secret #2: ASK

A primary means for seeing answered prayer—for noticing Godwinks—is to **ask**. This is revealed in the ancient Scriptures: "Ask and it will be given to you."

Secret #3: BELIEVE

Faith is critical to having our prayers answered, to seeing Godwinks. Faith comes from **believing** that God is who He says He is and that He can do what He says He can do.

Secret #4: EXPECT

The more you **expect** to be blessed by Godwinks and answered prayers, the more you will be able to see them.

Secret #5: SIGNS

During uncertain and trying times, God winks at you with **signs** that provide comfort and reassurance. Developing eyes to recognize the signs will increase your awareness of Godwinks and answered prayer.

Secret #6: WONDERS

Again and again in the ancient Scriptures, you will see God confirming His presence with signs and **wonders**. Your acknowledgment of the wonders He does in your life increases your ability to see them.

Secret #7: DIVINE ALIGNMENT

God **divinely aligns** us with other people so that we are at exactly the right place at exactly the right time, and He uses these Godwinks in the unfolding of His plan.